Sage One
FOR
DUMMIES®

by Jane Kelly, ACMA

WILEY

A John Wiley and Sons, Ltd, Publication

Sage One For Dummies®

Published by
John Wiley & Sons, Ltd
The Atrium
Southern Gate
Chichester
West Sussex
PO19 8SQ
England
www.wiley.com

For general information on our other products and services, please contact our Customer Care Department within the U.S. at 877-762-2974, outside the U.S. at 317-572-3993, or fax 317-572-4002.

For technical support, please visit www.wiley.com/techsupport.

Wiley publishes in a variety of print and electronic formats and by print-on-demand. Some material included with standard print versions of this book may not be included in e-books or in print-on-demand. If this book refers to media such as a CD or DVD that is not included in the version you pur-chased, you may download this material at http://booksupport.wiley.com. For more information about Wiley products, visit www.wiley.com.

British Library Cataloguing in Publication Data: A catalogue record for this book is available from the British Library

ISBN 978-1-119-95236-7 (pbk); ISBN 978-1-119-95375-3 (ebk); ISBN 978-1-119-95376-0 (ebk); ISBN 978-1-119-95377-7 (ebk)

10 9 8 7 6 5 4 3 2 1

About the Author

Jane Kelly trained as a Chartered Management Accountant while working in industry. Her roles ranged from Company Accountant in a small advertising business to Financial Controller for a national house builder. For the last few years Jane has specialised in using Sage accounting software and has taught a wide variety of small businesses and employees the benefits of using Sage. More recently Jane has been involved in writing *For Dummies* books, the first one being *Sage 50 For Dummies,* which continues to be a popular choice for Sage users. This latest book has been produced to explain the benefits of the Sage One service that has recently launched. Jane saw a gap in the market for providing a book that offers a Have a Go section where readers can use dummy data to try out the online accounting service.

Dedication

I would like to dedicate this book to my daughter Megan and my husband Malcolm. Without their support none of my books would ever have been created.

Author's Acknowledgments

I hope that this book will help many of the small business owners that currently struggle keeping up-to-date with their finances. I want people to understand that if a system is set up properly, it will be very easy to use and the business will gain maximum benefit from it.

I want to thank everyone at Wiley who have been very kind and supportive, particularly Rachael Chilvers and the rest of the development team who have turned my words and pictures into the *For Dummies* book that you see before you.

I would also like to thank the staff at Sage UK Limited, particularly Michael Barber and Richard Hughes, who have patiently answered my questions and comments about Sage One.

Finally, I would like to thank my husband Malcolm and my daughter Megan who have put up with me disappearing into the office to work on the book for what must have seemed like a never-ending time.

Publisher's Acknowledgments

We're proud of this book; please send us your comments at http://dummies. custhelp.com. For other comments, please contact our Customer Care Department within the U.S. at 877-762-2974, outside the U.S. at 317-572-3993, or fax 317-572-4002.

Some of the people who helped bring this book to market include the following:

Acquisitions, Editorial and Vertical Websites

Project Editor: Rachael Chilvers

Commissioning Editor: Claire Ruston

Assistant Editor: Ben Kemble

Development Editor: Andy Finch

Technical Editor: Richard Hughes

Proofreader: James Harrison

Production Manager: Daniel Mersey

Publisher: David Palmer

Cover Photos: © iStock / designalldone

Cartoons: Ed McLachlan

Composition Services

Project Coordinator: Kristie Rees

Layout and Graphics: Claudia Bell, Joyce Haughey

Proofreader: Melanie Hoffman

Indexer: Claudia Bourbeau

Publishing and Editorial for Consumer Dummies

    Kathleen Nebenhaus, Vice President and Executive Publisher

    Kristin Ferguson-Wagstaffe, Product Development Director

    Ensley Eikenburg, Associate Publisher, Travel

    Kelly Regan, Editorial Director, Travel

Publishing for Technology Dummies

    Andy Cummings, Vice President and Publisher

Composition Services

    Debbie Stailey, Director of Composition Services

Contents at a Glance

Table of Contents

Chapter 11: Entering Data into Your Cashbook 165

Part IV: Working with an Accountant 195

Chapter 12: When the Going Gets Tough: Calling an Accountant 197

Foreword

*A*ccounting has been around for thousands of years and still forms part of everyday business life. It's core to all businesses and is as important as any other process such as paying your staff or buying stock.

But you don't start a business because you want to produce accounts. You start a business because you have a passion for what you do and you want to achieve success. The accounting side is just a necessary part of the process.

When Sage was established in 1981, the emerging technology consisted of floppy disks and an Amstrad office computer. Out of that spirit of innovation came the first Sage software package designed to help businesses with basic accounting. These days, businesses have an ever-increasing choice when it comes to deciding on how to run their business and how to record their accounts. Some use spreadsheets; some prefer to do it manually using receipts and notebooks; while others use accounting software. And with computers and the Internet increasingly present, more and more people are using laptops, iPads and mobile phones to help run their business and are looking for the solutions to fit their needs.

We too have come a long way from those first floppy disks. Sage is now a global company. A leading supplier of business software to 6.3 million businesses worldwide. With over 30 years' experience of working with businesses of all sizes, we've continued to develop our accounting and business software. And in January 2011 we launched Sage UK's first online accounting solution – Sage One.

We talked to hundreds of small businesses and accountants all across the UK to find out what they needed from an accounting service. And our goal became delivering safe, simple online accounting, supported by the experts.

Sage One benefits from the advances in technology that have led to the introduction of *Software as a Service* – essentially, software that is run over the Internet or 'cloud', via an Internet browser. These cloud services offer many advantages to businesses. They're typically cheaper than their traditional desktop counterparts because there are no production or packaging costs. And because you can access them from Internet-enabled devices, such as PCs or Macs, iPads and even mobile phones, you're less restricted and can operate your business on the move.

We want to make it really easy for business owners to run their business using online services. We believe that necessary business processes, like accounting, shouldn't get in the way of you actually running your business. But because we recognise that the relationship between a small business owner and an accountant is important, we designed Sage One to allow them to work together easily, efficiently, online and in real time.

The aim of *Sage One For Dummies* is to help you maximise the value of using Sage One to manage your business finances. As Sage One requires no previous accounting knowledge there's a real synergy between Sage One and the *For Dummies* brand. *For Dummies* books take away the jargon and strip back complicated processes, making them easy for the inexperienced, which is exactly what Sage One is all about.

We understand that you didn't get into business to produce accounts. So, by making the necessary parts of the process as simple and straightforward as possible, you can get on and enjoy running your business.

Chris Stonehouse

Head of Sage Online, Sage UK Limited

Introduction

*M*ost people love running their own small business, but hate the idea of doing the paperwork. For example, although you know that you need to keep receipts, most of them are probably stuffed in envelopes or plastic bags waiting until your accountant asks for them.

A few business people may keep a spreadsheet detailing income and expenditure, but this format can all too easily become unwieldy to deal with.

Fortunately, here comes Sage One now, riding over the horizon to the rescue, enabling you to keep your records filed neatly online. The program can be accessed at any time of the day or night, and so you can see your financial data online and update it even in the middle of the night!

Accurate and complete financial records are crucial to any business owner, particularly when dealing with bank managers, asking for a loan or providing information to Her Majesty's Revenue and Customs (HMRC).

About This Book

In this book I show you how to setup, use and make the most of Sage One Accounts and Sage One Cashbook. I also discuss Sage One Accountants Edition, so that you know the benefits of this extra service for you and your accountant.

I provide step-by-step guides showing you how to:

- ✔ Prepare professional sales invoices very quickly and easily.
- ✔ Manage your cash flow.
- ✔ Record your purchase invoices.
- ✔ Prepare a simple Profit and Loss account and Balance Sheet.
- ✔ Prepare your VAT return.

In addition, I discuss the role of accountants within your business. You may already have one, but if not I help you determine whether employing the services of an accountant is appropriate for you and how to go about finding one.

Conventions Used in This Book

I use the Sage One service throughout this book, concentrating mainly on the Accounts service, but also discussing the Cashbook and the Accountants Edition. To help you find your way around the book, I use the following conventions common to all *For Dummies* titles:

- *Italics* indicate a defined term or a point of emphasis.
- **Boldfaced** text highlights the key phrase in a bulleted or numbered list.
- Monofont is used for web addresses.

In addition, where I need to use a gender-specific term in the text, for example when referring to accountants, I use female in even-numbered chapters and male in odd-numbered chapters, to avoid constantly using the clumsy 'he/she' or 'him or her'.

What You're Not to Read

The aim of this book is to get you confidently using Sage One as quickly as possible. I include lots of examples and exercises and also some practical bookkeeping tips on how to keep your financial records. Focus on those you find most useful. If you intend to use the full Sage One Accounts service and need to do VAT returns and send out invoices to people, you don't need to read Part III on the Cashbook.

In addition, if you want the basic info quickly, you can safely skip the text in grey boxes and anything marked with the Technical Stuff icon.

Foolish Assumptions

While writing this book, I made some key assumptions about you and why you picked up this book to get a better understanding of Sage One. I assume that you're one of the following:

- ✔ A business owner who wants to keep orderly accounting records. You have a good understanding of business and its terminology, but you don't have the time or inclination to tackle the full implications of bookkeeping and accounts.

- ✔ The spouse/partner of a sole trader who's been tasked with 'sorting out the accounts'. You need a simple and easy to understand system, so that you can accurately record the cash and cheques that flow in and out of the business. You also want to be able to hand over the records to your accountant in the most timely and cost-efficient way possible.

How This Book Is Organised

I organise *Sage One For Dummies* into five parts, which I outline below. I also include a Glossary at the back of the book, which highlights some of the bookkeeping terms that you may come across while running your business. You can dip in and out of it as and when the occasion arises.

I provide loads of opportunity for you to complete various exercises throughout the book, so that you can practise what I discuss in the chapter. By using the dummy data provided, you can set up customers, suppliers and bank accounts, enter sales and purchase transactions, and reconcile your bank account. You also produce a dummy VAT return. Just check your screens and reports against the ones I supply so that you can see whether you've got the hang of things and entered the data correctly. Alternatively, you can simply start entering your own data as soon as you've read the chapter.

Part I: Setting Up and Registering Sage One

In Part I, I show you how easy setting up and registering with Sage One really is. I explain the three variants of Sage One, which helps you determine the best one (excuse the pun) for your needs. In this part, you successfully set up your system and enter customer and supplier records, all ready to start receiving data.

Part II: Using Sage One Accounts

In Part II, I introduce Sage One Accounts and show you its features and benefits. You find out how to prepare professional looking sales invoices in minutes. You also discover how to enter your purchase invoices and bank transactions. I explain the importance of, and how to do, bank reconciliations, and from the data you enter, how to run your VAT Return, Profit and Loss account and Balance Sheet.

Part III: Introducing Sage One Cashbook

In Part III, I explain what the Sage One Cashbook can do for your small, probably cash-based, business. I talk about registering and setting up your Cashbook and I go into detail about how you enter your data. I show you how to handle income and expenses and which useful reports you can use for your business.

Part IV: Working with an Accountant

In Part IV, I discuss how an accountant can help you with your business. I explain the role that an accountant undertakes for your business and how one can help by offering advice on the best way to structure your business. I also look at the various different ways in which you can find an accountant.

I also talk about the Sage One Accountant Edition and explain how it works. I show how this service enables an accountant to help you with your accounts in several ways.

Part V: The Part of Tens

This part is central to all *For Dummies* books. I include a chapter on troubleshooting, which shows you how to resolve problems that you may experience as you use Sage One. I also share ten top tips for running your accounts system.

Icons Used in This Book

For Dummies books use little pictures, called icons, to flag certain chunks of text. The icons in *Sage One For Dummies* are:

 Look to this icon for ideas on how to improve your bookkeeping processes and manage your business accounts.

 This icon marks anything I really, really want you to recall about using Sage One, or even just good bookkeeping practice.

 This icon points out any aspect that comes with pitfalls or hidden dangers. I also use this icon to mark anything that can get you into trouble with HMRC, your bank or suppliers.

 This icon discusses some of the more complex aspects or offers some background. Feel free to skip these paragraphs if you prefer; you don't miss anything essential to using Sage One.

 Like all professions, the financial and accounting worlds use their own specialised terms. Although I keep these to an absolute minimum, where one is explained, I flag it for you with this icon.

 In these sections, I invite you to try out Sage One for yourselves using the dummy data that I provide. Wherever possible, I give you sample answers and reports to help you understand how to use the online service.

Where to Go from Here

I structure this book so that you can jump in anywhere and easily find what you need to know. For example, use the comprehensive Table of Contents or Index to look up specific topics. You can then follow the many cross references to other sections and chapters that contain related information. If you require a very simple Cashbook system and just want to keep a record of what's flowing in and out of your bank account, start with Part III on the Cashbook.

If you're completely new to Sage One, best to start at the beginning (how novel!) and read Part I first; these chapters describe the system and help you register, set up and create accurate opening balances. After that, go where you want. If a VAT return is looming, go straight to Chapter 8. If you want your accountant to join you in using Sage One as soon as possible, read Part IV next.

If you're still trying to decide which Sage One service to use, I suggest reading this Introduction (oh, you already are!) and Chapter 1. Then flip through the book to get an idea of what each of the three services offers.

Part I

Setting Up and Registering Sage One

'Now we've got all this money, we're going to need a sensible accounting system.'

In this part . . .

1 introduce Sage One and the three services that are provided, namely Sage One Accounts, Sage One Cashbook and Sage One Accountant Edition. By the end of this section you'll know how to successfully set up your system and will have entered some customer and supplier records.

Chapter 1

Introducing Sage One

*Y*ou may already be familiar with Sage and know that the company has been producing popular accounting software for some time. Perhaps you've used the well known Sage 50 software or Sage Instant Accounts. If so, you're probably wondering what Sage One is all about.

Sage One is unlike any other Sage service in that you use it entirely online. Therefore, you don't have to worry about discs to load or complicated installation schemes. As long as you have an Internet connection and a computer, you can access Sage One.

This chapter introduces you to Sage One, taking you through the product's benefits, available variants and navigation processes. I also guide you through online registration, which really is as easy as 1, 2, 3.

Meeting the Typical Sage One User

Sage One is designed for sole traders (one-person operations) and very small businesses. The service is intended for people who want to organise their finances in a more effective way than simply using a spreadsheet; for instance, business people who want to control their finances but don't necessarily have the accounting background or time for software training. With Sage One, you can be up and running very quickly, and yet still have the ability to allow your accountant (if you have one) to check the data held online.

Three forms of Sage One are available, as I discuss in the later section 'Acquainting Yourself with the Three Variants of Sage One', but as a user, you have only two options: the Cashbook and Accounts variants (the third type is for accountants).

Reading this introductory chapter gives you enough information to decide which variant best suits your needs.

Enjoying the Benefits of Sage One

Here are just some of the many benefits of using Sage One:

- ✓ Cheap to use – as little as £5 per month for Cashbook and £10 per month for Accounts.

- ✓ Quick to set up, and so ideal for small or startup businesses.

- ✓ No complicated software to install – you simply need to register (something I lead you through in the later section 'Registering for Sage One').

- ✓ 24/7 support available, and so if you decide to do your books in the middle of the night and get stuck, you know you can always get someone at the end of the phone to help you.

The fact that Sage One is an online accounting service means that you can work remotely from your office; you simply need an Internet connection and your laptop and you can work from anywhere. (Sage recommends you use an up-to-date browser.)

The online nature of Sage One ensures that you're always using the most up-to-date service, and you don't waste valuable time installing updates or new versions. The updates are made automatically online and you don't pay additionally for them.

Introducing cloud computing

Sage One uses *cloud computing* technology, which is a way of storing and accessing information in a web-based location. The data can be accessed, updated and maintained – and is secured remotely.

Cloud computing removes the need to back up large chunks of data in-house. All you need is an Internet connection and you can access your information anytime, anyplace, anywhere (as a well-known drinks company used to say).

Cloud computing isn't new, and has been used for accessing personal data for some time: think about accessing hotmail messages while away from home or making a purchase via PayPal.

Sage Pay is a fantastic example of how cloud computing works in practice. The system is completely online and the customers of over 31,000 businesses rely on it to buy goods over the Internet.

Sage One also allows your accountant to access your data quickly and remotely, enabling him to provide a more efficient service and perhaps pass on those savings to you as a client; or is that wishful thinking?

Sage One's tagline is 'Safe, Simple, Online Accounting':

- ✔ Safe, because the online security is taken very seriously.
- ✔ Simple, because the software is extremely easy to use.
- ✔ Online, because, well, as you know, it's online!

Acquainting Yourself with the Three Variants of Sage One

The three different types of Sage One are:

- ✔ Sage One Cashbook
- ✔ Sage One Accounts
- ✔ Sage One Accountant Edition

At the time of writing, a new variant is about to burst onto the scene – Sage One Payroll which will be a fully functioning payroll system.

This section looks at the basic features of each variant in turn.

Cashing in with Sage One Cashbook

Cashbook is a very simple service: a straightforward cash management module that, crudely speaking, allows you to manage the movement of cash flowing in and out of your bank account. You can also keep a record of all your customers and suppliers, managing all your contact details within your Cashbook.

The Cashbook program is ideal for small cash-based businesses who simply want to track their cash and provide some useful information, such as a Profit and Loss account.

To ensure the accuracy of your data, the service provides you with a bank reconciliation process, which allows you to check each individual transaction on Sage One against your bank statements, just to make sure that you've included everything.

You also have the ability to analyse your income and expenses and then produce a Profit and Loss report at the end of each month, which is calculated using the information that you entered.

 On the summary screen of Sage One Cashbook, a graph shows the bank balance over the period. This feature is useful for monitoring your cash closely (which in this economic climate is something everyone needs to be doing!).

Your accountant can access your Cashbook (provided he has the Sage One Accountant Edition, which I describe in the next section, 'Sharing data with Sage One Accountant Edition') and use your data to make corrections if you get into difficulties, or simply use the information to prepare your self-assessment tax returns and your VAT (if you're VAT registered).

Chapters 10 and 11 contain loads of details on using Cashbook.

Keeping track with Sage One Accounts

The Accounts variant contains more functions than the Cashbook service. Here are just some of the tasks that Sage One Accounts allows you to do:

- ✔ You can produce sales invoices and email them to your customers; this process is very quick and provides really professional-looking invoices in minutes!

- ✔ You can manage all your customer and supplier contacts online, creating records quickly and easily and then entering invoices as they're received from your suppliers.

- ✔ You can track your cash flow using the banking facility and prepare bank reconciliations to ensure that you've included all your transactions.

- ✔ You can produce a Profit and Loss account and a Balance Sheet, as well as a Trial Balance; usefully, your accountant can view your Trial Balance and use it to prepare statutory accounts if you so desire.

- ✔ You can calculate and submit your VAT return online.

As with the Cashbook service, if your accountant has the Sage One Accountant Edition he can access your data in real time, and therefore sort out any queries that you may have with your data and make the necessary adjustments. Your accountant can also use the data to produce your self-assessment returns or prepare your year-end accounts.

Turn to Chapters 4–9 for all about using Sage One Accounts.

Sharing data with Sage One Accountant Edition

This variant of Sage One allows your accountant to access your data and work collaboratively with you in real time, which means that any data you enter into Sage One is immediately available for him to see. Therefore, if you need help reconciling your bank account or preparing your VAT return, your accountant can have a quick look at your data and help you solve the problem.

Only accountants who purchase the Accountant Edition or are members of the Sage Accountants' Club (in which case, they get it for free) can access the appropriate software.

The more effective use of your accountant's time that the Accountant Edition provides should (in theory) lead to lower costs for yourself, as a client.

Your accountant can customise your income and expenses to make them more relevant to your business. He can also do journals, allowing you to get on with your day-to-day running of the business without having to get involved with the nitty-gritty of your accounting system.

Chapter 13 covers using the Accountant Edition in more detail.

Registering for Sage One

Sage allows you to try the service before you buy and register for a 30-day free trial. The following list guides you through the easy registration process:

1. **Go to** www.sageone.com **where you're presented with the Sage One homepage (as shown in Figure 1-1).**

   Three boxes are at the top of the page: one for Accounts, one for Cashbook and one for Accountant Edition. You can register for Sage One Accounts or Sage One Cashbook. For the purposes of this chapter, you're going to register for Sage One Accounts. If you want to see how to register for Sage One Cashbook, flip to Chapter 10.

2. **Click the More About Accounts box in the middle of the Sage One homepage.**

   Doing so loads up the Accounts page where you can discover more about the software.

3. **Scroll down the page; you see an option to Sign Up to Accounts.**

   Click this button to sign up **for a 30-day free trial**.

4. **Submit your basic business details, such as name and contact details, in the sign up form that opens.**

   Click Continue (see Figure 1-2).

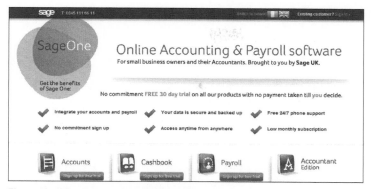

Figure 1-1: Viewing the Sage One homepage.

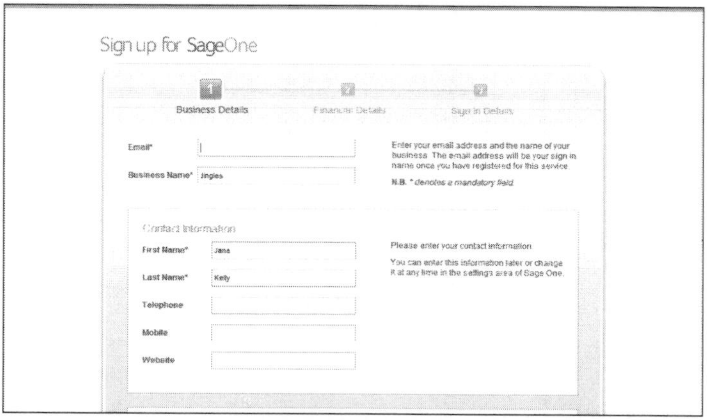

Figure 1-2: Completing your contact details during the registration process.

5. **Complete the basic requested details, such as your business address, accounts details and whether you're VAT registered.**

   If you answer yes to the VAT registration question, you need to identify which VAT scheme you use: for example, VAT standard rate, flat rate or cash accounting. Then click Continue (see Figure 1-3). You have the option of leaving this blank on sign-up and completing the details later.

Figure 1-3: Filling in your financial details.

6. **Supply a password in the now-displayed security details screen, and select three security questions and answers.**

   When you've agreed to Sage's Terms and Conditions, click the Complete Sign Up box.

7. **Click the link to activate the account when you receive the activation email.**

   You can now use your free version for 30 days (check out Figure 1-4).

Figure 1-4: Activating your Sage One service.

And that's it. You're ready to start using Sage One.

Navigating Sage One

When you've completed the registration process that I describe in the preceding section, you can start using Sage One. Log on to www.sageone.com, enter your email address and password, and click Sign In; the home screen then opens (as Figure 1-5 shows).

Figure 1-5: Signing in to Sage One.

The first screen you see is the Summary page (as shown in Figure 1-6), which displays your accounts data. Obviously to start with, it looks pretty blank and uninteresting!

Notice that the Summary screen is one of several tabs of information, the others being:

- ✔ Sales
- ✔ Expenses
- ✔ Banking
- ✔ Contacts
- ✔ More

Figure 1-6: Viewing the Summary screen.

In addition to the above tabs, which I describe in the section 'Checking out the Summary screen', the following three buttons are to the top right of the summary screen:

- ✔ Help
- ✔ Settings
- ✔ Sign Out

The Help button is very useful when you need to find out a bit more information about Sage One. For example, some video walkthroughs show you how to carry out certain tasks, such as setting up records.

Be prepared to keep pausing the video, because the videos whiz through the content at a rate of knots!

Turn to Chapter 2 for a detailed review of Settings.

When you finish using Sage One, simply click Sign Out to close down your Sage One session. Of course, the program saves the data you input.

Checking out the Summary screen

The Summary page is a graphical representation of the data that you input into Sage One. To the left of the screen, you have Sales to date, Expenses to date and Profit (all show the monthly figure and year to date). To the right of the screen, you have a graph showing the current bank balance over a specified time period. Below, you can find your top 5 unpaid sales invoices. These pieces of information indicate your cash flow, and how you can improve it by getting the money from your outstanding sales invoices.

Sales tab

This tab has three submenus:

✔ Sales Invoices

✔ Other Income

✔ Products and Services

Sales Invoices

You can use this screen to create new sales invoices, review existing ones and enter credit notes (as Figure 1-7 shows).

Figure 1-7: Viewing the Sales Invoices screen.

Other Income

Here you can record cash sales and any other income that you receive for which you don't need to generate a sales invoice (see Figure 1-8).

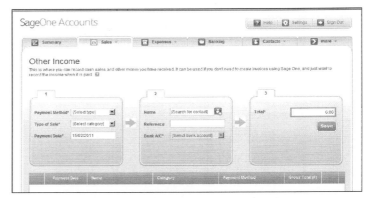

Figure 1-8: Looking at the screen where you can record Other Income.

Products and Services

Here you can create a product and/or service list so that you don't have to keep typing the same details into the invoice. When you come to raise your sales invoice, simply select the appropriate product or service record that you've created and a new line is created on your invoice without you continually having to type the details (see Figure 1-9).

Figure 1-9: Create new products and services using this screen.

Expenses tab

This tab has two submenus:

- ✔ Purchase Invoices
- ✔ Other Expenses

Purchase Invoices

Here you can record the purchase invoices that you receive from your suppliers, but haven't yet paid. You can also enter credit notes. If you're entering an invoice from a new supplier, you can create a new contact here (check out Figure 1-10).

Figure 1-10: Record purchase invoices using this screen.

Other Expenses

Here you can record cash payments that you make for which you don't have an invoice. You can choose from three different payment methods:

- ✔ Bank payment
- ✔ Cash payment
- ✔ Credit card payment

The payment method selected affects the bank accounts that are available to choose from on your dropdown menu. For example, if you click Cash payment you can use only the Cash in Hand account (see Figure 1-11).

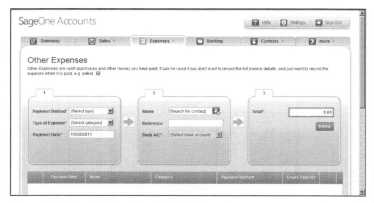

Figure 1-11: Showing the Other Expenses screen.

Banking tab

Under this tab you can manage all your bank accounts as well as Credit cards, Savings and Loans. Here you can create new bank accounts relevant to your business.

I often create a new bank account for petty cash, just so that I can keep an eye on what I spend from my petty cash tin.

You aren't restricted to only the two accounts given as default (see Figure 1-12).

Figure 1-12: Showing the two default bank accounts.

Contacts tab

The Contacts tab allows you to record and manage the details of both your Customers and Suppliers, as shown in Figure 1-13.

The two submenus are:

 ✔ Customers

 ✔ Suppliers

Figure 1-13: Showing the Contacts screen, where you can manage your contacts.

Customers

Use this screen to set up new customer records (see Figure 1-14).

Figure 1-14: Create new customers on this screen.

Suppliers

Set up new Supplier records here (as Figure 1-15 illustrates).

Figure 1-15: Create new suppliers on this screen.

More tab

Click this tab to gain access to the various reports that you can use (see Figure 1-16) as follows:

- Profit and Loss report
- Balance Sheet
- Transactional Trial Balance

✔ VAT return

✔ Outstanding Purchase Invoices

✔ Outstanding Sales Invoices

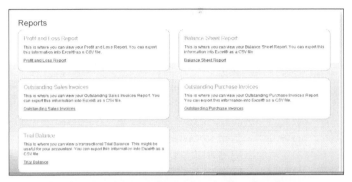

Figure 1-16: Showing the reporting options in Sage One Accounts.

Profit and Loss

Here you can view your Profit and Loss report (see Figure 1-17). You can also export this information to a CSV (comma separated value) file. CSV files are a particular type of format that can be accessed by most spreadsheet and database management software systems. For example, you or your accountant may want to take the data from Sage One and use another piece of software to analyse the data.

Figure 1-17: Showing the Profit and Loss report.

Balance Sheet

Here you can view your Balance Sheet report, but you can also export this information to a CSV file in the same way as the Profit and Loss report (as shown in Figure 1-18).

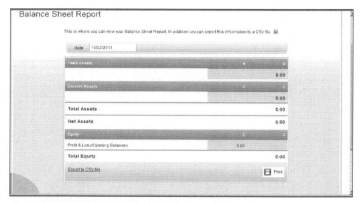

Figure 1-18: Showing the Balance Sheet report.

Transactional Trial Balance

Here you can view and print a Trial Balance, which your accountant can use to produce a set of accounts (see Figure 1-19). You can also print each report to PDF or export as a CSV.

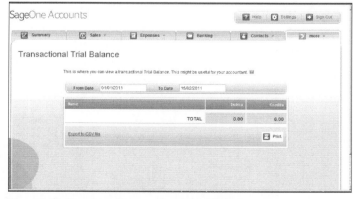

Figure 1-19: Showing a Transactional Trial Balance.

Introducing Jingles

The best way to find out how software such as Sage One works is simply to use it. Therefore, instead of messing about with your own information (although by all means get stuck in if you prefer!), I invite you to play around with some dummy data and see just what Sage One can do for you. To help with this approach, I use the fictional company *Jingles*.

Imagine that Jingles is a party planning company and Jeanette, the owner, has a shop from which she sells all sorts of party-related items. Throughout the book I use fictional records and transactions so that you can see how the Sage One software works and the kind of information that you can get from it.

You aren't obliged to use these 'have a go' sections and you can simply start using the system with your own data. The choice is yours.

Chapter 2

Sorting Out Your Settings

- -

In This Chapter

▶ Changing your personal settings

▶ Managing business and financial settings

▶ Checking that your settings are up to date

- -

*M*illions of people use Sage software and so necessarily the programs start off impersonal and generic. Therefore, making Sage One relevant and responsive to your particular needs is essential. Using the settings that Sage provides, you can personalise Sage One for your company and increase the direct usefulness of the service.

The settings are the backbone of the system, which is why I devote a full chapter to them; getting them right is a vital part of any accounting system. In this chapter I discuss Sage One's personal and business/financial settings. You discover why setting up and checking your VAT scheme (if you're VAT registered) as soon as possible is so important. I also guide you through making sure that you set up your invoices correctly for your business.

You need to enter your personal and business details *before* beginning to add any data.

Making Sage One Your Own: Creating Individual Settings

In this section, I show you how to set up your personal details on Sage One.

The Settings link appears at the top of every screen. Click this button and Sage One takes you to the Settings Overview screen, as shown in Figure 2-1.

Figure 2-1: Looking at the Settings Overview screen.

This screen contains two boxes of information. On the left side is My Sage One, which includes the following options:

- ✔ Billing Settings
- ✔ Service Settings
- ✔ User Settings

These screens enable you to set your personal settings and I look at each one individually in the following sections.

Paying up with Billing Settings

From the Settings Overview page, click Billing Settings and the following screen appears (see Figure 2-2).

Figure 2-2: Viewing your Billing Settings screen.

You see three tabs of information:

- ✓ Billing Contact
- ✓ Direct Debits
- ✓ Sage One Invoices

Billing Contact

In essence, this screen displays your personal contact details as shown in Figure 2-2. You complete most of this info on registering with Sage One (flip to Chapter 1 if you still need to carry out this process). If, however, you only fill in the bare minimum of detail at registration, you can complete your remaining details, such as your address and telephone numbers, using the Business Settings screen at a later point in time.

Direct Debits

The details of the direct debit instructions that you provide to Sage show here. You can see from Figure 2-3 that I haven't yet set mine up. (Sage will soon take debit or credit card payments rather than direct debit.)

Figure 2-3: Looking at your direct debit set up screen.

Sage One Invoices

This screen shows a list of all invoices received from Sage for the Sage One service (see Figure 2-4). Nothing is yet shown for Jingles (the fictional company I introduce in Chapter 1).

Figure 2-4: Viewing your Sage One Invoices on Billing Settings.

Deciding on your desired Service Settings

This screen shows the services to which you subscribe, and also confirms that you're signed up to the free trial service (a process I discuss in Chapter 1). Also note the Invite Accountant button on the right side of your screen (check out Figure 2-5).

Figure 2-5: You can invite your accountant using your Service Settings screen.

When you click this button, a new Invite Accountant window appears and you're asked to enter the email address of your accountant, as shown in Figure 2-6. Sage One then sends a message to your accountant's Sage One Accountant Edition service, notifying that you want to invite her to be your Sage One Accountant. When she accepts your invitation, your accountant can get direct access to your live data.

Figure 2-6: Using Sage One to send an invitation email to your accountant.

You can invite an accountant in this way only when she's already a Sage One accountant. She needs to be a member of the Sage Accountants' Club (who are automatically given access to Sage One service) or else make a payment to get access to the Sage One service. If your accountant doesn't use Sage One, but you want her to have access to your Sage One service via an Accountant Edition, please ask her to call Sage on 0845-111-1111.

Using User Settings

Here, you can change your password. Click the Change Password link to do so (see Figure 2-7).

Figure 2-7: Viewing your User Settings.

Taking Control With Your Business and Financial Settings

In this section, I describe how to set up your vital business and financial information including VAT and invoice details.

Look to the right side of the Settings Overview screen and see a box entitled Sage One Accounts, which includes the following options:

- Business Settings
- Financial Settings
- Invoice Settings

Displaying Business Settings

This screen contains the contact details for your business, which you can enter and update, including name, address and telephone numbers as well as your website address (see Figure 2-8); essential if you ever want customers to get in touch!

Figure 2-8: Viewing your contact details on the Business Settings screen.

Getting the VAT right: Financial Settings

This screen shows you your year-end date and selected VAT scheme. You can set your opening balances from this screen and also export data. As Figure 2-9 shows, I choose the standard VAT scheme for the fictional company Jingles (check out Chapter 1 for Jingles info) and note that Jeanette plans to submit the VAT return on a quarterly basis.

Figure 2-9: Viewing your Financial Settings.

At the time of registration (read Chapter 1 for details), you have to say whether you're registered for VAT. If you answer Yes, the system asks which VAT scheme you want to operate. Using a dropdown arrow, select the VAT scheme that you use.

Sage One stores this data in Financial Settings. If you want to change your VAT scheme at any point in the future, you need to do so via the Financial Settings screen.

Sage One offers the following current VAT schemes:

- ✔ Standard VAT (currently at 20%)
- ✔ Flat rate invoice based
- ✔ Flat rate cash based
- ✔ VAT cash accounting

Standard rate

The current standard rate of VAT is 20%. You charge VAT on all goods and services that are considered to be a taxable supply when you make a sale (called *output tax*). You can reclaim the VAT you pay to suppliers (called *input tax*). The difference is paid or reclaimed from or to HMRC.

The VAT Guide (Notice 700) is your bible when determining what you charge VAT on and what you can reclaim. See www. hmrc.gov.uk for further information.

Flat rate VAT scheme

HMRC allows you to calculate your VAT payment as a flat percentage of your turnover. The percentage is determined according to your trade sector. You can't claim any VAT back on your purchases and this scheme is only valid if your annual sales are less than £150,000.

The flat rate is calculated on a *cash basis* or an *invoice basis*. The flat rate scheme has its own cash-based method for calculating the turnover.

Read HMRC's VAT notice 733 for further details.

VAT cash accounting

If you use the VAT cash accounting scheme, your business accounts for income and expenses when they're actually incurred. Thus you don't have to pay HMRC until your customers pay you.

You're eligible to use this scheme if your turnover is not more than £1,350,000.

Using the Jingles dummy data, update the Financial Settings using the following information:

> Financial year-end: 31 March 2011
>
> VAT scheme: Standard VAT at 20%

Your screen now looks like Figure 2-9 (shown in the previous section).

Getting paid: Invoice Settings

Click Settings in the top right corner of any screen and then Invoice Settings, as shown in Figure 2-10.

From the Invoice Settings page, you can carry out a number of tasks to personalise the layout of your invoices:

- ✔ You can view and alter the Invoice Template, which is a preview of how your invoice is going to look.
- ✔ You can change or add your company logo.
- ✔ You can change or add association logos.
- ✔ You can amend invoice options.

I now look at each of these tasks in turn.

Altering your Invoice Template

Click Settings and then choose Invoice Settings.

If you want, you can see a preview of the current Invoice Template in use. To discover what other templates are available, click Change Template. The screen shown in Figure 2-11 opens, displaying a preview of the default template selected and three other template options.

Choose the one you want by clicking the desired template. The revised Invoice Template appears on the right in large view. If you like what you see, click Save. A confirmation message appears saying that you changed the template setting successfully.

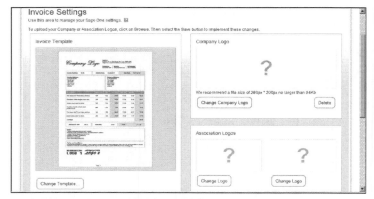

Figure 2-10: Viewing your Invoice Settings.

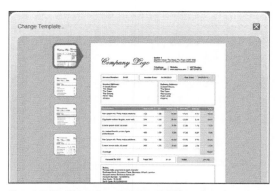

Figure 2-11: Changing your Invoice Template

Changing your company logo

From the main Sage One Homepage, click Settings and then choose Invoice Settings.

On the right side of the screen, click the Change Company Logo button. A new box opens with an option to browse for your logo (see Figure 2-12). Click this browse button and select the file that you want to upload. Double-click your file, and then click Save. A confirmation message appears confirming that you updated the image successfully. Your logo now appears in the logo box where previously had been a question mark. (Unless your logo is a question mark, of course, in which case it's now a different question mark!)

Change Company Logo

We recommend a file size of 280px * 200px no larger than 64Kb

Browse...

Save

Figure 2-12: Browsing for your company logo.

When you've made the necessary changes to your logo, click Save on the Invoice Setting page. A confirmation message appears saying that you updated your settings successfully, and you're returned to the Settings Overview page.

Sage can't load any image larger that 64K, so keep your file size less than this size. Sage recommends a file size of 280 x 200 pixels.

Changing association logos

If you have any association logos – for example, you're a builder who belongs to the Federation of Master Builders – you can add them here (assuming you have a copy of the logos, of course). From the Invoice Settings page, click the Change Logo button in the Association Logos screen. The Change Logo box opens, as shown in Figure 2-13.

Click the browse button and select the association logo file from your hard drive. Double-click that file and then click Save. A confirmation message appears saying that you saved the image successfully.

Figure 2-13: Browsing for your association logos.

If you don't belong to an association but do have a Facebook account, why not put a Find Us on Facebook type logo.

When you've made the necessary changes to your association logos, click Save on the Invoice Setting page. A confirmation message appears to confirm successful updating and you're returned to the Settings Overview page.

Amending Invoice Options

Scroll down to the bottom of the Invoice Settings page until you see the Invoice Options section (see Figure 2-14).

Figure 2-14: Viewing your Invoice Options.

Here you have the ability to enter some Terms and Conditions to appear on the face of your invoice. For example, you can type 'Payment within 30 days of date of invoice'.

To the right of the screen you can see:

- ✔ Customer Credit Days (30)
- ✔ Supplier Credit Days (30)
- ✔ Next Invoice Number

✔ Sales Invoice Number Prefix

✔ Sales Credit Note Number Prefix

Customer and Supplier Credit Days

These settings affect the default due date on invoices. The due date is automatically entered on the invoice if you enter credit terms within the Settings menu. You can, however, overwrite this date when recording an invoice if necessary.

Next Invoice Number

This setting is important when you're using Sage One with an existing business. Naturally, in such a case, you don't want Sage to start invoicing from number 1; instead, you need to specify the next invoice number in sequence, which may be, say, '3234' if you've been trading for some time.

Sales Invoice Number Prefix

What you input here appears before the sales invoice number: in this case 'SI-'. Therefore, invoice number 1 is printed as 'SI-1'.

Sales Credit Note Number Prefix

What you input here appears before the Sales Credit Note number. For example, Sales Credit Note number 2 is viewed as 'SCN-2'.

You can amend the Sales Invoice Number Prefix and the Sales Credit Note Prefix to whatever suits your business.

Using a Checklist

If you're like me and already have enough pieces of information floating around your brain, you may well find that a checklist is a very useful way to ensure that you've completed all the necessary tasks. Here's a checklist of all the things that you need to remember when setting up Sage One:

1. **Make sure that your VAT is set up correctly. Have you chosen the appropriate scheme?**

2. **Check the next invoice number that you need to use, if you don't intend to start from no 1.**

3. Upload your invoice logo and any association logos that you may want to add to your invoice.

4. Make sure that you've entered all your company details, such as name and address, in Settings.

You can't enter your opening balances for unpaid invoices unless you've set up all your company details.

Chapter 3

Keeping in Contact: Setting Up Your Records

*W*hen you're registered with Sage One (see Chapter 1) and happy with your business and financial settings (as I describe in Chapter 2), you can begin entering some records, including all your customer and supplier details. (After all, no point leaving all those fields empty!) I lead you through the various processes of entering, locating, amending and deleting records in this chapter.

I'm sure that you're champing at the bit to begin putting in your own data, but for now take a look at the Have a Go exercise in the later section 'Entering customer contacts', where I use the dummy data for the fictitious company Jingles (which I introduce in Chapter 1).

You soon see that setting up customer and supplier records is easy, leaving you to concentrate on raising invoices and get the money rolling in!

Sage One sees your customers and suppliers as *contacts*. Therefore, the Contacts screen (unsurprisingly) allows you to create and manage your list of contacts. Although you can view separate lists of your customers and suppliers, Sage One lists them all together on the Contacts screen to allow you to see them at a glance.

Creating Customer Records

Setting up customer records for Sage One is a very simple process, and when done, all your customers show as a list on the main customer screen.

Entering customer contacts

In this section, you discover how to enter customer contact details from the dummy example that I provide in the next Have a Go paragraph. (If you feel ready, of course, jump straight into using your own customer records.)

Jeanette owns Jingles, a party planning shop. She sells balloons, cards, party cakes, banners – practically anything you can imagine needing for a party. A lot of her sales are taken at the till and are therefore cash or credit card sales (I look at these transactions in a little more detail when I discuss banking in Chapters 6 and 10). However, Jeanette also invoices some customers and these people's details are shown in Table 3-1.

Table 3-1

Jingles Dummy Customer Details

	Customer Record 1	Customer Record 2	Customer Record 3
Name:	Mrs T Johnson	Paul Davis	Viv Richards
Company:	Johnson's Hire	Davis Dinners	Balloon Madness
Address:	73 Church Way	7 Brookfield Way	3 High Street
	Ashbourne	Buxton	Whaley Bridge
	Derbyshire	Derbyshire	High Peak
	DE43 6BY	SK17 2SL	SK13 6TY
VAT No:	Not VAT registered	564 7765 76	435 9876 55
Telephone:	01332 675438	01298 65478	01663 567876
Mobile:	07934 675489	07986 657456	07976 325476
Email:	tjohnson@googlemail.com	paul@davisdinners.co.uk	viv@balloonmadness.co.uk
Website:	www.johnsonhire.co.uk	www.davisdinners.co.uk	www.balloonmadness.co.uk

Please follow these steps to input the names, addresses, contact details and so on shown in Table 3-1:

1. **Sign into Sage One** (www.sageone.com).

2. **Click the Contacts tab from the main Summary screen, and then select Customers.** You can then click the Create Customer button to begin setting up your Customer records (see Figure 3-1).

Figure 3-1: Showing the screen where you can create customer records.

3. **Enter the contact details first, including contact name, company name, email address and telephone numbers.** To continue with the address details, click the link for Address and more fields drop down, allowing you to enter the address.

Further dropdown fields are available to enter a delivery address if different from the main address already entered. Also you can access the Notes field to add additional details such as a website address or details of office opening times and so on; whatever you feel is pertinent to that customer. You can, of course, leave the Notes field blank. Figure 3-2 shows a completed customer record prior to saving.

When you're happy with the details, click Save. As you do so, a confirmation message flashes up saying that you saved the contact successfully (see Figure 3-3).

Sage then takes you to the Customer screen, which shows a list of your customers; currently the one you just set up and

HMRC, because in Chapter 2 you set up Jingles as a VAT-registered company.

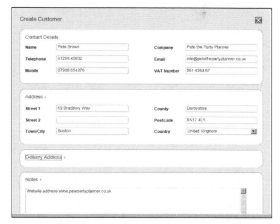

Figure 3-2: A completed customer record for Pete Brown.

Figure 3-3: Another contact is successfully saved!

When you've entered all your customer records, the screen looks something like the one in Figure 3-4.

Figure 3-4: Showing your list of Customers.

Sorting customer records

You can sort your entered customer records in different ways.

To sort your customer records into alphabetical order, simply click the grey shaded area with the word Name in it; doing so sorts the records alphabetically. You can sort the records in any order that you want. For example, you can sort them by telephone number, which may be useful if you want to contact customers within a specific area code. Alternatively you can sort them by email address, although I'm not quite sure how useful that would be!

Recording Supplier Details

After carrying out the exercise in the preceding section, you've had some practice entering customer records. Easy, isn't it? Now I turn to creating some supplier records. Suppliers in this context are people from whom you buy goods or services, and as such you need to record the invoices that they send you. But before you can record the invoices, you need to set up a supplier record for them.

Entering supplier records

You create supplier records in much the same way as customer records (see the earlier section 'Entering customer contacts').

If you have your own data to use, by all means go ahead and enter it. If, however, you want a little practice first, please feel free to use the dummy data supplied in the exercise below.

Please set up supplier records using the information provided in Table 3-2.

Table 3-2	Jingles Dummy Supplier Details		
	Supplier Record 1	*Supplier Record 2*	*Supplier Record 3*
Name:	Peggy Dickson	Richard Mather	Paul Page
Company:	Brilliant Balloons	Dagenham Party Supplies	P Diggories & Son
Address:	65 Edgeware Rd	Dagenham Industrial Estate	4 Brown Lane
	London	Priory Road	Chapel en le Frith
	NW3 6FG	Dagenham	High Peak.
		DG76 4KH	SK13 6TY
VAT No:	456 7765 87	532 6654 78	454 6754 88
Telephone:	0121 456547	01534 675987	01298 546786
Mobile:	04563 765897	06765 765976	07976 675438
Email:	sales@brillballoons.co.uk	ales@dps.co.uk	info@diggories.co.uk
Website:	www.brillballoons.co.uk	www.dps.co.uk	www.diggories.co.uk

Here are the steps to take:

1. **Sign into Sage One** (www.sageone.com).

2. **Click the Contacts tab from the main Summary screen, and then select Suppliers.** You can then click the Create Supplier button to begin setting up your Supplier records.

3. **Enter the contact details first, including contact name, company name, email address and telephone numbers.** To continue with the address details, click the link for Address and more fields drop down, allowing you to enter the address.

Use the further dropdown fields to enter a delivery address, if different from the main address already entered, and the Notes field to add additional details such as a website address or details of office opening times and so on. Enter anything you feel is pertinent to that supplier, or leave blank. Figure 3-5 shows a completed supplier record prior to saving.

Figure 3-5: A completed Supplier record for Paper Products Ltd.

Happy with the details? If so, click Save and see the confirmation message flash up to confirm that the contact is saved successfully.

Sage now takes you to the supplier screen, which shows a list of your suppliers: currently, the one you just set up and

HMRC (because Jingles is a VAT-registered company) – see Figure 3-6.

Figure 3-6: Showing the current list of Supplier records.

When you've finished entering the supplier records, your screen looks similar to the one in Figure 3-7.

Figure 3-7: A more comprehensive list of Suppliers.

Sorting your supplier records

Of course, you can sort your entered supplier records in all sorts of ways. To sort your suppliers alphabetically, simply click the grey shaded area with the word Name in it. This sorts the list of suppliers in alphabetical order. You can also click the header of the other grey shaded columns and sort the records by telephone number or even email address!

Tracking Down a Contact

From time to time you may need to search for one of your contact records quickly. The search method is the same whether you're looking for customers or suppliers. Simply hover your cursor over the Contact tab and select the appropriate customer or supplier from the menu.

Imagine that you want to search for Johnson's Hire in the customer records. From the customer list, you begin typing Johnson's in the *Type the contact name to search* box. Sage One automatically lists all the customer records that begin with John. In fact I only got as far as typing John before the computer found the record I was looking for (see Figure 3-8).

You can now highlight to open up the Johnson's Hire record, and so read or edit the details.

Figure 3-8: Searching for a customer.

Editing Your Contact Details

You can edit customer and supplier contacts in the same easy way as finding a contact (see the preceding section 'Tracking Down a Contact'). Start from the Contact screen:

1. **Click the customer or supplier that you want to edit.** Doing so opens up the customer or supplier record.

2. **Click the Manage Customer or Manage Supplier button, to the right of the screen.** A dropdown menu appears. Select Edit and you can now change whatever information you desire. For example, the email address may require updating.

3. **Click Save at the bottom of the screen when you've made the changes.** A confirmation message appears confirming that you've made the changes successfully.

Deleting Contacts: You're Outta Here

You can delete contacts records when necessary, although you can't delete contacts with outstanding transactions.

Deleting is a very simple process, starting from the Contact screen:

1. **Click the grey cross next to the contact that you want to delete.**

2. **Read the confirmation message that appears asking whether you're sure that you want to delete that contact.**

3. **Click Yes to delete or No to return to the Contact Summary screen.**

HMRC (Her Majesty's Revenue and Customs) Contacts

When you state that you're a VAT-registered company at the point of registration or you subsequently change your financial settings to say that you are VAT registered, Sage One automatically creates two contacts when you sign up.

✔ **HMRC Payments:** When you create and save your VAT return, and Sage One calculates that you owe the HMRC some money, Sage One automatically creates a purchase invoice against the HMRC payments supplier. The invoice equates to the value of VAT owed and can be paid off in the normal way. See Chapter 5 for paying suppliers.

✔ **HMRC Reclaimed:** If you're fortunate enough to generate a VAT reclaim while saving your VAT return, Sage One automatically creates a sales invoice for the value of the VAT reclaim. You can then apply the bank receipt against the sales invoice in the normal way.

Producing Product/ Service Records

Product and service records help you quickly prepare invoices based on the type of products you sell or services that you provide.

Jeanette, the owner of the fictional party company Jingles, has services and products, and so she needs to create records for both. Turn to Chapter 4 to find out how to create product records, which is where I cover entering your opening balances. I also refer to this subject in Chapter 5 when I show you how to create sales invoices.

Banking That Income: Creating New Bank Records

Sage One provides you with two banking accounts as a default: Current and Cash in Hand. You can create a new bank account from the Banking tab or when you're entering your opening balances (I discuss opening balances in Chapter 4.)

Open a new account from the Banking screen as follows:

1. **Select the Banking tab from the main toolbar.** The Banking screen opens with two default bank accounts already set up: Current and Cash in Hand.

2. **Hover over the Manage Bank Accounts button; a dropdown menu appears.** Click the Add a New Account link. The new account window opens as shown in Figure 3-9.

3. **Enter your new bank account name, number and sort code, and select the type of account using the dropdown menu.** You can choose Current, Savings, Credit Card, Loan or Other accounts. You can also add the address and contact details of your bank, if you want.

4. **Click Save when you're happy with the details you entered.** Your new account appears on the Banking Summary screen.

Figure 3-9: Creating a new bank account.

Chapter 4

Recording Your Opening Balances

*I*n this chapter, I describe how to enter your opening balances in Sage One. Before entering them, however, note that you need to have set up your records first – turn to Chapter 3 for how to do so.

Entering your opening balances is crucial because they represent the financial position of your business on the day that you start using Sage One. You probably have opening balances even if you've just started up; for example, perhaps you already opened a business account and have a few initial transactions.

You need to enter the opening balances accurately because they form the basis of your accounts; if they aren't correct, neither are your subsequent accounts. Just imagine the future problems you can avoid by getting the entries right at this stage!

Entering Your Opening Balances

In order to prepare to enter your opening balances, you need the following information to hand:

- ✔ **Bank statements:** Use these to find your bank balance on the date prior to starting Sage One. For example, if you're entering transactions from 1 April 2011, you need your bank balance as at 31 March 2011 as your opening bank balance.

- ✔ **Outstanding Sales Invoices:** You may have a list of these known as an Aged Debtor report.

- ✔ **Outstanding Purchase Invoices:** This list is often known as an Aged Creditors report.

If you're changing from one accounting system to another, you may well be able to print off a Trial Balance as at the closing prior period. This report is ideal if you can obtain it. Otherwise just use the three items in the preceding list.

When you've gathered the required information together, follow these steps starting from the Sage One homepage:

1. **Click Settings, and then Financial Settings.** Figure 4-1 displays the screen.

Figure 4-1: Accessing Opening Balances.

2. **Click the Opening Balances link at the bottom of this screen.** Figure 4-2 shows the relevant screen.

Figure 4-2: Entering the Start date.

3. **Input the last day of the previous financial year on the Opening Balances screen, and then click Next to continue.** The bank details screen opens, as shown in Figure 4-3.

Figure 4-3: Entering bank opening balances.

4. **Enter your bank balance in the box provided.** If you need to enter more than one bank account, or perhaps you have a bank loan or a credit card for which you need to set up an opening balance, click New Account. Figure 4-4 shows an example of setting up a new credit card on Sage One.

Figure 4-4: Entering a credit card as a new bank account.

5. **Click Save when you're happy with the new details.**
A confirmation message pops up on the screen saying that you've set up the account successfully. The new account now shows on the opening balances screen (see Figure 4-5).

Figure 4-5: Showing the new Credit Card account set up.

6. **Click Next to continue.** The Unpaid Invoice screen opens (check out Figure 4-6). You can now record any purchase or sales invoices that were unpaid at the date you entered on the first screen in step 3.

7. **Click Save.** Of course, do so only when you're happy with the entered details.

Figure 4-6: Entering Unpaid Invoices.

 In order to enter sales invoices as opening balances you must have already set up some contacts in Sage One. Flip to Chapter 3 to find out how.

Creating Products and Services for Unpaid Sales Invoices

When you're creating unpaid sales invoices on your opening balance screen, you need to create products and/or services. I lead you through this process in the following list of steps, starting from the Unpaid Invoice screen I describe in step 6 of the preceding section:

1. **Click Record Sales Invoices.** The New Sales Invoice screen opens as shown in Figure 4-7.

2. **Enter the name of the customer in the Name field.** Sage One helpfully provides you with a dropdown list of all available customers.

3. **Select the appropriate customer.** If the customer contact isn't listed, click the little person icon (the Create Contact button) to the right of the Name field and the Create Customer box opens.

4. **Input your customer details and click Save (see Figure 4-8).** A confirmation message appears saying that you've set up the customer record successfully.

The customer account details now appear in the new Sales Invoice screen.

Figure 4-7: Creating a new product for an unpaid invoice.

Figure 4-8: New Customer details entered.

5. **Choose to create a product or a service, depending on whether your business supplies products or services (obviously!).** I'm dealing with a product for this example and so click the Create Product button so that the Create Product box opens.

6. **Enter the details for Happy Birthday helium balloons.** Check out Figure 4-9.

Figure 4-9: Creating a helium balloon product record.

7. **Input an Item Code for the product.** Basically, this code is used to identify each product; in this case enter 'Helium-HB' (HB being Happy Birthday).

   Creating meaningful codes is much more useful than just entering numbers.

   After entering the item code, you need to give the product a description, as a further means of identification.

8. **Click Type of Sale and choose Sales or Other Income.** Other Income implies anything other than your normal business products, for example, bank interest. If neither of these options suit, you can choose the **Create New** link and a new window opens, enabling you to create a new sales type or other income type (if VAT-registered, enter a VAT rate when creating new products or services).

9. **Add any required additional notes about the** product in the Notes section. I add a note to say that the balloons are foil-covered. You can leave this blank if your product description is sufficient. In addition, you can enter the cost price and the sales price of the item.

10. **Click Save when you're happy with the details you've entered.** A confirmation message appears on the screen saying that the product is set up successfully. The details of the product you entered now appear on the new sales invoice.

Check that the quantity details and the prices are correct before saving the details (see Figure 4-10). Overtype the amounts where possible.

Figure 4-10: An extract of a new sales invoice.

11. **Click Save when you're happy with the invoice details.** A confirmation message confirms that you've successfully saved the new opening balance. The invoice now appears on the Unpaid Invoices screen (as shown in Figure 4-11). Repeat steps 1–8 and enter all your unpaid sales invoices.

Figure 4-11: The Unpaid Invoice list.

Recording an Unpaid Purchase Invoice

In the preceding sections, I describe how to record unpaid sales invoices. As you may guess, entering unpaid purchase invoices is very similar.

You can enter your purchase invoices from Step 3 of the opening balances wizard. Then simply follow these steps:

1. **Click Record a Purchase Invoice.** The new Purchase Invoice screen opens as shown in Figure 4-12.

Figure 4-12: Recording an Unpaid Purchase invoice.

2. **Search for your purchase contact.** Create a new one using the Create Contact button, if you can't locate the correct contact (see Figure 4-13). Click Save and the contact details appear on the new Purchase Invoice screen.

Figure 4-13: Recording a new supplier.

3. **Make sure that the date is correct on the invoice.** If so, enter the description of the invoice. For example, 500 sheets of wrapping paper.

4. **Select the expense type by using the dropdown arrow (as shown in Figure 4-14).** Sage One provides a default list of codes.

If this list is unsuitable for your business, you can click the Create New link, and a new window opens, enabling you to create a new expense type. Your accountant can edit or remove these expense types by using the Accountant Edition of the Sage One software. (Chapters 1 and 2 contain more on the Accountant Edition.) For the purposes of this exercise, I use Cost of Sales – Goods.

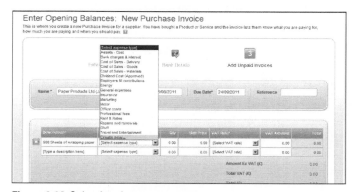

Figure 4-14: Selecting the expense type.

5. **Enter the quantity and unit price concerned.** Notice that the VAT is calculated automatically on the invoice. Add more lines to your invoice if you have additional items (check out Figure 4-15).

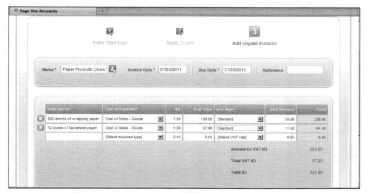

Figure 4-15: Additional products added to the purchase invoice.

6. **Click Save when the invoice details are correct.** A confirmation message tells you that the purchase invoice is set up successfully. The unpaid purchase invoice now appears on the same list as the unpaid sales invoices (as shown in Figure 4-16).

Figure 4-16: Unpaid invoice list showing both unpaid sales and purchase invoices.

7. **Click Save when you're happy with all your unpaid invoices that form your opening balances.** A confirmation message confirms that you've saved your opening balances successfully. You're then returned to the Financial Settings screen.

Running Through Some Exercises

The preceding sections give you all the information you need to create your opening balances. If you want a bit more practice, however, work through the following exercises.

Again, I use the fictional party company Jingles. Answer the following questions using the processes I describe in this chapter:

1. **Create an opening bank balance as at 31 March 2011, for £250, for the Buxton Bank Current account.** You need to rename the existing current account to read Buxton Bank Current account.

2. **Using the following details, create a new bank account for the credit card:**

   Account name: Carrot Credit Card

   Account number: 4567 34456 4567 2345

   Account type: Credit Card

   Account balance: –£123.45

3. **The two sales invoices in Table 4-1 are outstanding at 31 March 2011.**

   Using Table 4-1, create the sales invoices. You need the following information to set up the product records for Invoice 1:

   Happy Birthday Helium Balloons:

   Stock code: Helium-HB

   Sales Price: £2 each

   Cost price: £1

Using Table 4-1, create another sales invoice and use the following information to create the product records for Invoice 2:

Snowman Christmas Cards:

> Stock code: Snowcard

> Sales price: £1

> Cost price: 50p

Happy Birthday Cute Bear Cards:

> Stock code: Cards – HBCuteBear

> Sales price: 75p

> Cost price: 35p

Party Poppers:

> Stock code: Partypop

> Sales price: £2 per box

> Cost price: £1

Table 4-1   Sales Invoice Details for Exercise 3

	Invoice No 1	*Invoice No 2*
Customer details:	Pete the Party Planner	The Village Shop
	69 Bradbury Way	5 Main Street
	Buxton	Ticknall
	Derbyshire	Derbyshire
	SK17 4LY	DE73 2YT
Date of invoice:	21 March 2011	25 March 2011
Invoice details:	20 Happy Birthday helium balloons	20 Snowman cards
		15 Happy Birthday cute cards
		10 Party Poppers

4. The purchase invoices in Table 4-2 are outstanding at 31 March 2011.

Using Table 4-2, enter two purchase invoices, one from Paper Products Ltd and the other from Derby Wholesale Cards.

Table 4-2 Purchase Invoice Details for Exercise 4

	Invoice No 1	*Invoice No 2*
Supplier details:	Name: Josie Smith	Name: Davina Bradbury
	Company: Paper Products Ltd	Company: Derby Wholesale Cards
	Address: Nashville Trading Estate	Address: Risedale Industrial Estate
	Ashbourne	
	Derbyshire	Derby
	DE6 7FG	DE3 6JF
	VAT No: 565 7654 77	VAT No: 654 7777 43
	Telephone: 01332 675876	Telephone: 01332 543876
	Mobile: 07654 564387	Mobile: 06754 678543
	Email: info@paper products.co.uk	Email: info@dwc.co.uk
	Website: www.paper products.co.uk	Website: www.dwc.co.uk
Date of invoice:	1 March 2011	13 March 2011
Invoice details:	Supply of 500 sheets of wrapping paper @ £199	10 Variety packs of Birthday cards @ £64.00
	12 boxes of handmade paper@ £87	10 packs of Get Well Soon cards @ £28.00
	Their invoice no: 5467	10 packs of assorted 'Cute Cards' @ £25.00
		Their invoice no: 4536A

If you want to confirm your answers to the Have a Go exercises, check out Figures 4-17 to 4-19. For the sake of space, rather than show you both sales Invoices 1 and 2, I just show you an extract of sales Invoice 2, so that you can see the layout, but you can check your totals for each invoice using Figure 4-19 which shows all the invoices that have been entered.

Figure 4-17: Confirmation of opening bank balances for Jingles.

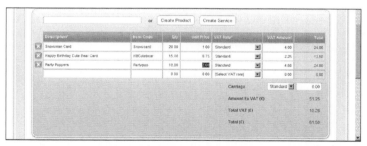

Figure 4-18: Extract of Customer Invoice No 2 for the Village Shop, showing details of all the invoiced products.

When you've entered your opening balances, you're ready to start adding some transactions, a process I describe in Chapter 5.

Figure 4-19: Invoice list showing all unpaid invoices set up.

Part II
Using Sage One Accounts

'Mr Scrimshaw, our acccountant, was schooled in the old manual way but I'm sure you two will enjoy working together on a new computerised system.'

In this part . . .

1 introduce Sage One Accounts and show you the features and benefits of this service. You'll discover how easy it is to create professional sales invoices in minutes! You'll also see how to enter purchase invoices and bank transactions, which leads you to performing bank reconciliations simply and easily. Finally you'll find out how you can quickly run VAT returns and financial statements such as the Profit and Loss and Balance Sheets.

Chapter 5

Entering Invoices for Customers and Suppliers

In This Chapter

▶ Creating sales invoices

▶ Viewing, editing and voiding your sales invoices

▶ Producing credit notes

▶ Entering purchase invoices

*I*n this chapter I lead you into the nitty-gritty of the Sage One system. Here's where you start using the system to produce some really professional looking invoices in a very short space of time. I also look at how to create credit notes and why you may need to raise them. As well as looking at the sales documentation, I also show you how to record your purchase invoices easily and conveniently.

Getting Paid: Setting Up Sales Invoices

Cash is king for a business, and unless you're a cash-based business (such as a shop) you need to raise invoices to your customers to start the money rolling in!

You need to have your own business address set up before you can raise sales invoices (a process that I describe in Chapter 2). If you haven't already done so, please click Settings and then Business Settings to enter this info now.

Here's how to raise invoices for your customers:

1. **Click the Sales tab from the Summary screen.** Select Sales Invoices from the menu.

2. **Click the Create Invoice button and the New Sales Invoice screen opens.** Enter the name of your customer in the Name field. As you do so, notice that Sage provides you with a dropdown list of the possible customers. Figure 5-1 shows how to find a customer record.

Figure 5-1: Finding a customer record.

If you're creating an invoice for a new customer, and you don't already have a customer record set up, simply click the icon of the little person with the plus sign to take you to the New Customer Record screen.

3. **Enter the invoice date by clicking the Date box and using the calendar function provided.** The due date is calculated based on the customer credit days that you've entered in your Invoice Settings. The default is set to 30 days. Alternatively, you can simply type in the date.

4. **Input a reference (using the Reference field) if you want to – perhaps an order number.** If you don't have a reference, leave this field blank.

5. **Tick the small box at the bottom of the screen if the delivery address is to be the same as the main**

address. Otherwise, enter the address of where you're going to deliver the goods.

6. **Enter the product or service for which you intend to invoice.** To use an existing product or service, simply begin to enter the item concerned.

   If no matches come up, you have to create a product or service by clicking the Create Product or Create Service button and completing the boxes. (Chapter 4 contains all the details on how to create a new product or service.) Creating an invoice simply gives you another way to create these items.

   I assume in this case that the product shows on your list and the product information appears in the New Sales Invoice screen.

7. **Click the Description to add more details to the invoice.** You can change the number of units sold by clicking the Quantity column. The sales price is already there, but you can overtype the amount if you need to change it.

8. **Use the dropdown arrow to select the VAT rate applicable for the invoice.** Figure 5-2 shows the different VAT rates available. Sage One automatically calculates the VAT amount on the invoice. You can add an additional charge for carriage if required.

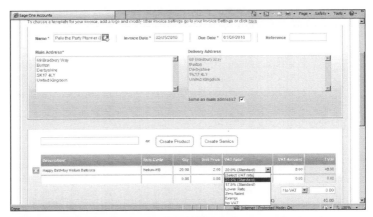

Figure 5-2: Selecting the appropriate VAT rate for your sales invoice.

9. **Add additional Notes if you want, such as 'Delivery can be left next door with the neighbour'.** You can also enter terms and conditions here, such as 'Payment due 30 days from date of invoice'. Doing so helps when you come to collect the money from the customer.

10. **Place a tick in the relevant box to choose whether you want to print or email the invoice.** Click Save.

    A confirmation message appears saying that you've saved the invoice successfully.

 The invoice now appears on the Sales Invoice list. Notice the invoice has automatically been allocated an invoice number ('SI' stands for Sales Invoice). You can override this invoice number if you aren't a business start up. Check out Chapter 2 for how to use Settings to do so.

Working With Sales Invoices

In this section, I discuss some of the tasks you can perform when you've created a sales invoice (as I describe in the earlier 'Getting Paid: Setting Up Sales Invoices' section).

Viewing and editing a sales invoice

To view the invoice, navigate to the Sales tab and select Sales Invoices. Doing so brings up a list of your Sales Invoices. Click the sales invoice that you want to view; once the invoice has appeared on the screen you can select to Print, Edit or Email via the Manage Invoice button or create a credit note.

Figure 5-3 shows an unpaid invoice in Edit mode.

 When you've created products and services for your invoices, for future invoices simply click the Search for a Product or Service box next to the Create Product or Create Service button and type your product description. Sage immediately provides you with a dropdown list of all products and services available, and you simply point and click to select the one you want.

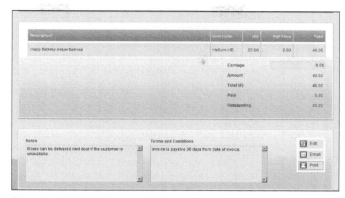

Figure 5-3: Click Edit to view the invoice.

You can edit an existing unpaid invoice by clicking the invoice from the Sales Invoice list. Doing so opens up the invoice, and by highlighting the Manage Invoice button, then selecting Edit, you can amend any details you want.

Voiding a sales invoice

If you find that you make a mistake on your invoice, you can easily void it (not as unpleasant as it sounds!) with the following very simple process:

1. **Click the small cross next to the invoice on the Invoice List screen.** A new window opens as shown in Figure 5-4.

Figure 5-4: Voiding a sales invoice.

2. **Enter the reason why you require the invoice to be voided and then click Save.** The payment status of that invoice is now described as Void, but the invoice doesn't disappear from view and remains on the invoice list for audit purposes.

Sage doesn't alter the sequential invoice numbering system, so that if HMRC decide to inspect your records, they find no missing gaps in your invoice sequence. The only thing apparent is a note of voided invoices, much as you void a cheque and write the same in your cheque stub. Invoices which have been included on the VAT return cannot be voided

And that's it: invoice voided. I did say it was simple!

You cannot void an invoice where you have recorded a payment or credit note against it, or if it has already been included on a VAT Return.

Entering a discount for a sales invoice

You can easily enter a discount to a sales invoice by adding a separate line to the invoice and using the word 'discount' to describe the item. Then enter the amount as a negative number. You also need to apply a VAT rate to the discount using the dropdown list. Sage then recalculates the amount the customer owes. Figure 5-5 shows how to enter a discount on a sales invoice.

Description	Item Code	Qty	Unit Price	VAT Rate	VAT Amount	Total
Party Poppers	Partypop	22.00	2.00	Standard	8.80	52.80
Place Settings - Heart	Placeseth	50.00	1.00	Standard	10.00	60.00
Discount		1.00	-9.40	Standard	-1.88	-11.28
		0.00	0.00	[Select VAT rate]	0.00	0.00

Carriage	Standard	0.00
Amount Ex VAT (£)	84.50
Total VAT (£)	16.92
Total (£)	101.52

Figure 5-5: Entering a discount for a sales invoice.

Printing your sales invoice

Unless you email them (something I describe in the following section), you're going to want to print your invoices in order to post them out.

To print out an invoice, simply follow this procedure:

1. **Hover over the Sales tab and click Sales Invoices. From the invoice list, select the invoice you want to print by clicking once.** The invoice opens up.

2. **Scroll down the invoice.** Check the details as you go to ensure that everything is correct.

3. **Click the Manage Invoice button and select Print from the menu.** *Voila:* a beautifully presented invoice, done in double-quick time!

Figure 5-6 shows a copy of a completed invoice.

Emailing your sales invoice

Instead of printing an invoice and posting it, you can email the invoice as soon as you create it. Just think of how much more environmentally sound this option is! Not only are you saving a small piece of the planet, but also saving money on postage and, more importantly, time.

The sooner the customer gets the invoice, the sooner you get paid.

When you create an invoice, here's how to email it:

1. **Tick the Email box at the bottom of the invoice and then click Save.** Doing so opens up a separate window, where you find the email address already selected.

   Figure 5-7 shows how you can add your own personal message.

2. **Click Send to email the invoice to your customer.** They can open it as a PDF file.

Email is instant and so a really great way of quickly sending invoices to your customers.

If you want to email an invoice on your invoice list, you need to use the Manage Invoice button and select Email from the menu. The email address only appears if you've entered it on the contacts record.

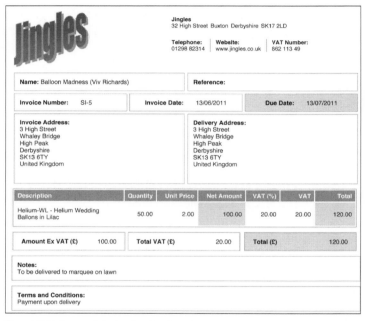

Figure 5-6: A completed sales invoice.

You can always follow up the email with a phone call to make sure that the customer receives it (and you're re-emphasising that the invoice is due for payment as well).

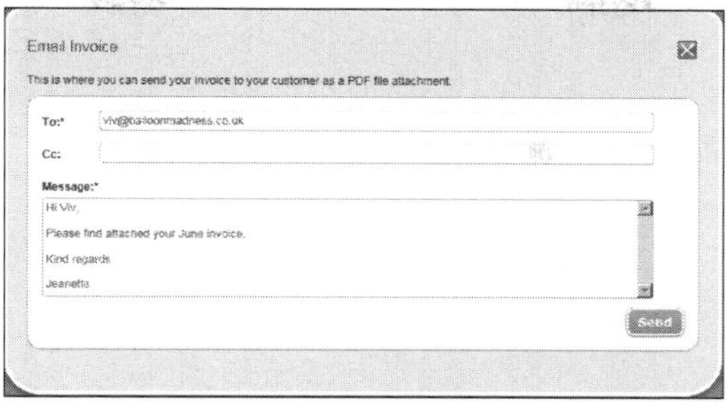

Figure 5-7: Emailing a sales invoice.

Giving Credit Where It's Due: Raising a Credit Note

All sorts of situations may require you to create a credit note, usually because an invoice or part of an invoice is wrong and needs correcting. For example, assume the customer orders 12 boxes of cards but 12 boxes of place settings arrive instead. Your business needs to raise a credit note for the invoice sent for the incorrect products, and send a new invoice with the correct order.

Whatever the reason, the credit note reverses the effect that an invoice has on the Sage One system. To raise a credit note, please follow these instructions starting from the main toolbar:

1. **Hover the cursor over the Sales tab and select Sales Invoices.** You're presented with the list of sales invoices.

2. **Select the invoice against which you want to raise a credit note.** You can now view that relevant sales invoice.

3. **Hover over the Manage Invoice button and select the Create Credit Note option on the dropdown list, which appears as shown in Figure 5-8.**

Figure 5-8: Using the Manage Invoice button to create a credit note.

A new window opens up, as shown in Figure 5-9, displaying the details of the original sales invoice, although the heading now shows Credit Note. The date automatically defaults to today's date (you may want to change this).

Figure 5-9: Creating a sales credit note.

4. **Amend the details of the credit note as desired.** You can use the Notes section at the bottom to add the reason for the credit note being raised.

If you want to email the credit note, click the Email box – doing so opens up a new window – and email the credit note. (Check out the earlier section 'Emailing your sales invoice' for all the necessary details.)

5. **Click Save.** Of course, only when you've entered all the information and are happy with it.

You can view a saved credit note from the Sales Invoice list – it appears with the reference 'SCN' in the invoice number column. The amount is a negative value and the screen displays a default status as Paid (check out Figure 5-10).

Sometimes you need to create a credit note against just part of an invoice instead of against the whole thing. For example, perhaps you want to raise a credit note for only one of several products on your invoice.

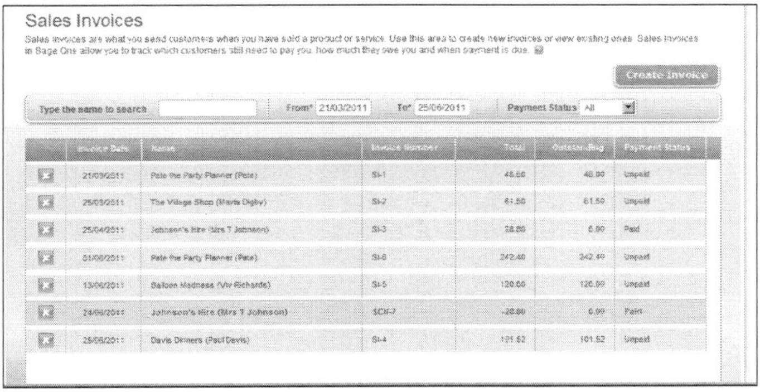

Figure 5-10: The credit note in the Sales Invoice list.

Assume that sales invoice no 4 has two different products on it:

22 Party Poppers at £2 each

50 Heart-shaped place settings at £1 each

The client receives both products, but isn't happy with the place settings. A credit note is therefore required to deduct the cost of the place settings. Here's how you produce one:

1. **Follow steps 1–3 in the preceding list.** Open sales invoice no 4 to create a credit note.

2. **Delete the items as necessary, leaving only the items for which you want to create a credit note.**

If a discount is applied to the original invoice, you have to delete this line and net any discount off the product line, because Sage One doesn't like negative values on a credit note.

3. **Click Save when you're happy with the credit note.**
Sage One confirms that you've saved a new credit note successfully and it appears on the Sales Invoice list (as shown in Figure 5-11). Notice that the credit note says Paid against it, but invoice no 4 has Part Paid against it, because the credit note is allocated against only part of the invoice.

Sales Invoices

Sales Invoices are what you send customers when you have sold a product or service. Use this area to create new invoices or view existing ones. Sales Invoices in Sage One allow you to track which customers still need to pay you, how much they owe you and when payment is due.

Create Invoice

Type the name to search		From* 21/03/2011	To* 25/08/2011	Payment Status All

	Invoice Date	Name	Invoice Number	Total	Outstanding	Payment Status
	21/03/2011	Pete the Party Planner (Pete)	SI-1	48.00	48.00	Unpaid
	25/03/2011	The Village Shop (Mavis Digby)	SI-2	81.50	81.50	Unpaid
	25/04/2011	Johnson's Hire (Mrs T Johnson)	SI-3	28.80	0.00	Paid
	01/06/2011	Pete the Party Planner (Pete)	SI-6	242.40	242.40	Unpaid
	13/06/2011	Balloon Madness (Viv Richards)	SI-5	125.00	125.00	Unpaid
	24/06/2011	Johnson's Hire (Mrs T Johnson)	SCN-7	-28.80	0.00	Paid
	25/06/2011	Davis Dinners (Paul Davis)	SI-4	101.52	47.52	Part Paid
	25/06/2011	Davis Dinners (Paul Davis)	SCN-8	-54.00	0.00	Paid

Figure 5-11: A credit allocated against part of an invoice.

Recording Purchase Invoices

In this section, I show you what to do when a supplier sends you an invoice.

You need to record all invoices in your accounting system, preferably as soon as they arrive into the business. That way, you can see what liabilities you've incurred.

To enter your purchase invoices, please follow these steps:

1. **Hover over the Expenses tab from the main Summary screen and then select Purchase Invoices.**

2. **Click Record Invoice from the Purchase Invoices screen.**

3. **Click the Name field and enter the supplier name for which you want to record an invoice.**

4. **Enter the date of the invoice: the due date is calculated based on the information you enter in the Invoice Settings screen (flip to Chapter 2 for more details).**

5. **Enter a reference in the Reference field (see the nearby sidebar for a helpful tip).**

6. **Click the Description box, and enter the details of the invoice.**

7. **Select the expense type using the dropdown arrows; you're given a series of options as shown in Figure 5-12.** If you want to create a new expense type, simply click Create new.

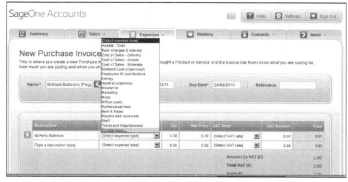

Figure 5-12: Entering a purchase invoice into Sage One.

Keeping count of purchase invoices

I use a sequential numbering system for all my purchase invoices – starting from number 1 and so on. I can then file the invoices in a single lever arch file rather than having numerous files with suppliers recorded in alphabetical order. Sage One has a useful reference field, which I use to record my own sequential number, with the supplier invoice number in brackets. This approach is always useful when you're discussing your supplier's account with them, because you have a cross reference with your invoice number and theirs.

8. **Select the Quantity and Unit Price.**

9. **Check that the net amount of the invoice agrees with the purchase invoice in your hand, and confirm the VAT amount is correct.**

10. **Click Save, when you're happy that you've recorded the details correctly.**

A confirmation message appears saying that you've successfully saved the purchase invoice.

The purchase invoice now appears on the Purchase Invoice list, displaying a status of unpaid as shown in Figure 5-13.

Figure 5-13: The Purchase Invoice list.

Recording a Supplier Credit Note

Just as you sometimes have to raise a sales credit note to correct a sales invoice, so your suppliers may find that they have to do the same.

Here's how you record a credit note you receive from a supplier, starting from the Purchase Invoice list:

1. **Hover over the Manage Invoice button and select Create Credit Note. The credit note opens ready for editing or saving.**

Adding a reason

Although no separate field is available, if you want to add a reason for issuing the credit note, you can amend the description line and add some more detail. For example, you can add that the wrong colour was ordered.

2. **Click the Create Credit Note button in the top right corner of the invoice when you've opened up the correct purchase invoice.** Doing so opens up a new Credit Note window for your supplier, but it still contains all the details of the original invoice.

3. **Amend the credit note to show the correct details.** (The nearby sidebar contains a useful trick.)

4. **Click Save when you're happy that the details of the credit note are correct (make sure that you have the correct date and any reference number).** A confirmation message appears on the screen to say that you've successfully created a credit note.

The credit note shows as a negative value on the purchase invoice list, with a status of Paid marked against it. The invoice for which the credit note is allocated also shows an amount credited against the total value of the invoice.

Trying Out Some Invoice Exercises

To get used to just how easily you can enter sales and purchase invoices and their corresponding credit notes, have a go at the following examples.

1. **Enter a sales invoice using the following information:**

   Customer: Mrs T Johnson (contact details are the same as those shown for this contact in Chapter 3)

Invoice no: 3

Date of invoice: 25 April 2011

10 Wine Bags at £2 each (see below for product details)

2 Party Poppers at £2 each (this product was set up in Chapter 4)

Product details:

> Wine Gift Bag (Item Code: Winebag)
>
> Cost: £1
>
> Sales Price: £2

Have a look at Figure 5-10, which shows the Sales Invoice list with these items on it.

2. **Enter a purchase invoice using the details below:**

Supplier: Brilliant Balloons

Invoice date: 23 May 2011

Our invoice no: 3

Invoice details:

> 100 Helium Party Balloons at £1 each
>
> 100 Helium Wedding Balloons at £1 each
>
> 10 packets of assorted party balloons at £12

Please use expense type: Cost of Sales Goods

Their invoice no: 113

Payment terms: 30 days from date of invoice.

To check that you've entered the details correctly, see Figure 5-14.

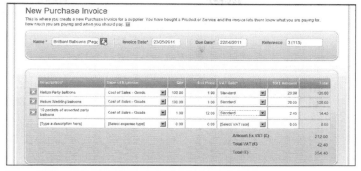

Figure 5-14: Brilliant Balloons Purchase Invoice no 3.

3. **Enter the following Sales Credit Note:**

   Credit note to: Mrs T Johnson

   Date: 26 June 2011

   Reason for credit: Client not happy with the goods

   Credit required for full value of invoice no 3

   Description: To credit invoice no 3

   Refer to Figure 5-10 to see the credit note showing in the Sales Invoice list.

4. **Enter the following Purchase Credit Note:**

   Credit note from: Brilliant Balloons

   Date: 25 May 2011

   Reason for credit: Assorted party balloons credited

   Description: To credit invoice 113

   You can see this credit note in Figure 5-15.

Figure 5-15: The credit note raised for Brilliant Balloons.

To see a list of all the purchase invoices, including those entered as opening balances, take a look at Figure 5-16.

Figure 5-16: A list of Purchase Invoices entered into Sage One.

Chapter 6

Recording Payments from Customers and to Suppliers

. . . .

In This Chapter

▶ Entering payments from customers

▶ Checking and refunding sales invoices

▶ Settling up with suppliers

▶ Using the Outstanding Sales and Purchase Invoice reports

. . . .

*O*ne of the best bits of being in business is getting paid by your customers! Filling in your paying-in slips and putting money into your bank account is really gratifying and makes all the hard work seem worthwhile. In this chapter I look at how to record a payment when a customer sends you some money. I also describe the less enjoyable but no less important task of recording payments that you make to your suppliers.

Recording a Customer Payment

You've received a customer payment – yippee! Before you can consider how to spend it (paying bills, probably), you have to record the amount. Here's how:

1. **Hover on the Sales tab and then click Sales Invoices.**
   From the Sales Invoice list, click the invoice to which you want to allocate the customer receipt. Doing so enables you to view the invoice.

2. **Click the Record Payment button in the top right corner of the invoice.** A Record Payment window opens, as shown in Figure 6-1, where you need to enter the following details:

   – The amount paid

   – The date received

   – Whether the payment is to be paid into the Current account or Cash in Hand

   If the payment is a cheque, tick the relevant box. You also need to give the payment a reference, such as the paying-in slip reference number.

Figure 6-1: An example of recording a payment in Sage One.

3. **Click Save when you've checked that the details are correct.** A confirmation message appears saying that you've made the payment successfully.

The screen still remains in invoice viewing mode. You can see a box at the top of the screen showing that a payment has been made against the invoice, as shown in Figure 6-2.

Scroll down the invoice: notice that the invoice now says that it has been paid and the amount outstanding is zero, as shown in Figure 6-3.

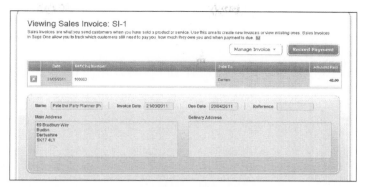

Figure 6-2: A payment allocated against a sales invoice.

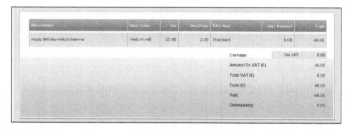

Figure 6-3: An extract of a sales invoice showing the balance outstanding as zero.

When you return to the Sales Invoice list, you see that the status of the invoice is now Paid.

The above process is fine if the customer pays the correct amount, but life isn't always so straightforward, and sometimes customers don't pay the correct amount for an invoice. And yet, when you click Record Payment, Sage One assumes that you're recording a payment for the full value of the invoice and automatically defaults to that amount.

If the payment is for the wrong amount, you need to allocate the exact amount that the customer pays. Simply overtype the amount that you received in the Record Payment box.

Then follow the rest of the steps above for recording a payment.

Recording batch payments

You can also record batch payments to pay multiple invoices in one go. To record a batch payment, hover over the invoices you want to pay and click the box that appears next to the payment status column. Click the Record Batch Payment link that now appears to the top right of the screen:

A new window opens called Record Batch Payment as shown in the following figure. Enter the date and cheque number and which bank account you're paying it into. Tick the box if you received a cheque. Click Save, and a confirmation message appears saying that the payment has been successful.

Note: You can only record multiple payments from the same customer. You can also apply payments to multiple supplier invoices in a similar way, but only to the same supplier.

The difference is that if you scroll down to the bottom of the invoice, it still shows that an amount is outstanding and the Sales Invoice screen says that the invoice has been part-paid.

Handling Other Customer Payment Tasks

In this section, I describe how Sage One can help you keep track of customer payments.

Running an Outstanding Sales Invoice report to check who's paid

Sage One provides an easy method to check who has paid you and – perhaps more important – who hasn't. You can run an Outstanding Sales Invoice report (also known as an Aged Debtors report), which shows you a list of unpaid sales invoices, split into 30-, 60- and 90-day periods.

The usefulness of the Outstanding Sales Invoice report depends on how up to date your records are. Ideally, running this report forms part of your monthly routine; the best time is when you've reconciled your bank account, because then you can be sure that you've allocated all the payments from your customers. I talk about the bank reconciliation process in Chapter 7.

You can use an Outstanding Sales Invoice to help you collect in the money from your customers:

1. **Click the More tab from the main screen. Select Reports.**

2. **Click the Outstanding Sales Invoices link.** A new window opens up showing you a list of outstanding invoices in columnar format, arranged from current to older than 90 days, as shown in Figure 6-4.

Figure 6-4: Outstanding Sales Invoices on the screen.

3. **Click the View the Detailed Report link: a new window opens and the report can be reviewed on the screen in PDF format.** You can choose to print or save a copy of the PDF file to a location on your computer.

   You can also hover over the Download Report button and two further options appear:

   – Printable PDF: This produces a neat report (an example is shown in Figure 6-5).

   – Export to CSV File: CSV (comma separated values) is a particular type of file format, which can be used to move tabulated data between different computer programs that support compatible CSV formats. For example, you can use a CSV file to transfer information from a database program to a spreadsheet.

4. **Click Export to CSV File.** A new window opens as shown in Figure 6-6.

5. **Click OK to open the file within Microsoft Excel.** You can now view the data in Microsoft Excel as shown in Figure 6-7; it can be manipulated and turned into any sort of report you desire.

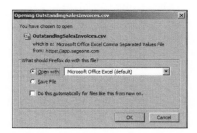

Outstanding Sales Invoices

Date 28/06/2011

Customer	Total	0 to 30 days	31 to 60 days	61 to 90 days	Older
Balloon Madness (Viv Richards)	120.00	120.00	0.00	0.00	0.00
Davis Dinners (Paul Davis)	47.52	47.52	0.00	0.00	0.00
Pete the Party Planner (Pete)	242.40	242.40	0.00	0.00	0.00
The Village Shop (Mavis Digby)	10.25	0.00	0.00	0.00	10.25
Total	£420.17	£409.92	£0.00	£0.00	£10.25

Figure 6-5: The Outstanding Invoice report shown as a printable PDF file.

Opening OutstandingSalesInvoices.csv

You have chosen to open

OutstandingSalesInvoices.csv

which is a: Microsoft Office Excel Comma Separated Values File
from: https://app.sageone.com

What should Firefox do with this file?

◉ Open with   Microsoft Office Excel (default)
○ Save File

☐ Do this automatically for files like this from now on.

OK   Cancel

Figure 6-6: The Export to CSV File window.

	A	B	C	D	E	F	G	H	I	J	K	L	M
1	Customer	Total	30 Days	60 Days	90 Days	Older							
2	Balloon Madness (Viv Richards)	120	120	0	0	0							
3	Davis Dinners (Paul Davis)	47.52	47.52	0	0	0							
4	Pete the Party Planner (Pete)	242.4	242.4	0	0	0							
5	The Village Shop (Mavis Digby)	10.25	0	0	0	10.25							
6	All Journals	0	0	0	0	0							
7	Total	420.17	409.92	0	0	10.25							

Figure 6-7: Viewing the Outstanding Sales Invoice data in Microsoft Excel.

An alternative to running the Outstanding Sales Invoice report is to check the Sage One Summary tab. If you scroll down to the bottom of the page, you see the Top 5 Unpaid Sales Invoices, giving you a snapshot of your business's debtors. However, if you have 20 debtors, this information is of limited use, because you can't view them all.

Refunding an invoice

You may find yourself in a situation where you have to refund a sales invoice. (I describe creating sales invoices in Chapter 5.)

Here's how to apply a refund, starting from the main toolbar:

1. **Hover over the Sales tab and select Sales Invoices from the menu.**

2. **Select the invoice that you want to refund from the Sales Invoice list – whether it's a part or full refund – and the invoice opens in a new window.**

3. **Click the Record Payment button at the top right side and the Record Payment window opens.**

4. **Enter the amount you want to refund against the invoice as a negative figure (check out Figure 6-8 to see an example of how this looks).**

Figure 6-8: How to apply a refund to a sales invoice.

5. **Click Save when you're happy with the refund details.**

The refund payment is saved and recorded against that invoice. It also displays in the Record Payment box.

Paying Up: Recording a Supplier Invoice

In order to keep your suppliers happy, you need to pay them on time! To do so, complete the following steps:

1. **Hover over the Expenses tab.** Select Purchase Invoices from the dropdown menu.

2. **Click the invoice you want to pay from the Purchase Invoice list.** You can now view that invoice.

3. **Click the Record Payment button in the top right of the invoice screen.** The record payment window opens as shown in Figure 6-9.

4. **Enter the following information:**

   – The amount paid (this figure defaults to the total invoice value, but you can overtype it if paying only part of an invoice as I describe in the next section 'Paying part of a supplier invoice').

   – The date that you paid the invoice.

   – Which account you're paying out from; for example, your current account or perhaps a credit card account.

   – Reference or cheque number, as shown in Figure 6-9 (I recommend that you use the cheque number so that you can easily match it off when you come to reconcile the bank account).

5. **Click Save, when you're happy that the entered details are correct.** A confirmation message appears saying that you've made the payment successfully.

Figure 6-9: Recording a supplier payment.

The screen remains in invoice viewing mode. A box appears at the top of the screen showing that a payment has been made against the invoice, as shown in Figure 6-10.

Figure 6-10: A payment box appears when you've paid a supplier invoice.

Scroll down the invoice and you can see that it has been paid and the amount outstanding is zero.

Paying part of a supplier invoice

Sometimes you may want to part-pay an invoice; perhaps you agreed with the supplier to pay in stages. In this case, follow Steps 1–3 in the preceding section, but when you get to Step 4, simply enter the amount that you're actually paying. You need to overtype the amount, because Sage assumes that you're paying the whole amount.

Carry on with the rest of the steps as shown above.

Paying off more than one invoice

Often, when you're paying suppliers, you'll find that you want to pay more than one invoice to the same supplier. In order to save time, Sage One has developed a method of paying off more than one invoice at a time. Here's how:

1. Click the Expenses tab and then the Purchase Invoices link. This opens up the Purchase Invoice list. You can identify which invoices remain unpaid by scanning your eye down the Payment Status column.

2. To indicate which invoices you want to pay, hover your mouse over each of the unpaid or part-paid invoices, and click the small box that appears to the right of the payment status column.

3. Click the Record Batch Payment link that appears to the top right of the screen, and this opens the Record Batch Payment window. Fill in the details requested and click Save.

4. A confirmation message appears saying that the payment has been successfully made.

When you've saved the part payment, you can scroll down to the bottom of the invoice and confirm how much has been paid against this invoice and the balance still outstanding, as shown in Figure 6-11.

Figure 6-11: A part-paid supplier invoice

Notice that on the Purchase Invoice list the status of the invoice shows as part-paid.

Producing an Outstanding Purchase Invoice report

Running this report is helpful when you need to check who you owe money to.

As with the Outstanding Sales Invoice report (which I describe in the earlier 'Running an Outstanding Sales Invoice report to check who's paid' section), this report is only really of any real use if you keep your records up to date and regularly reconcile your bank account (something I cover in Chapter 7).

The Outstanding Purchase Invoice report shows you which invoices are currently unpaid and ranks them in chronological order so you can see how long the invoices have been outstanding for.

To run the report, please follow the steps below:

1. **Click the More tab.** Select Reports from the dropdown menu.

2. **Click the Outstanding Purchase Invoices link.** The relevant screen opens showing a list of unpaid invoices, as shown in Figure 6-12.

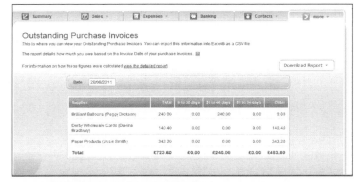

Figure 6-12: Outstanding Purchase Invoices on the screen.

3. **Choose to click the view the detailed report link that opens up a new PDF window showing the report.** Or you can click the Download Report button on the right side of the screen.

The instructions for using the Download Report are the same as I describe in the earlier section on 'Running an Outstanding Sales Invoice report to check who's paid'.

Getting in Some Practice

This section offers you the opportunity to practise some of the things I discuss in this chapter. For the following situations, carry out the necessary tasks. Doing so helps you fully understand how to use the software.

1. **Enter the following customer cheque received on 31 May 2011:**

   A cheque arrives from Pete the Party Planner for £48. Jeanette pays this into the bank. The payslip reference is 100006 and the cheque is for payment of Sales Invoice 1.

   Figure 6-1 shows the payment received.

2. **Enter the following customer cheque received on 1 June 2011:**

   Jeanette receives a cheque from The Village Shop for £51.25. Unfortunately she forgot about the VAT element and so you can't pay the invoice in full. The payslip reference is 100007.

   Figure 6-13 shows an extract of The Village Shop invoice after the part payment has been allocated.

Description	Item Code	Qty	Unit Price	VAT Rate	VAT Amount	Total
Snowman Card	Snowcard	20.00	1.00	Standard	4.00	24.00
Happy Birthday Cute Bear Card	HBCutebear	15.00	0.75	Standard	2.25	13.50
Party Poppers	Partypop	12.00	2.00	Standard	4.00	24.00
			Carriage	Standard	0.00	
			Amount Ex VAT (£)		51.25	
			Total VAT (£)		10.25	
			Total (£)		61.50	
			Paid		-51.25	
			Outstanding		10.25	

Figure 6-13: A part-paid invoice for The Village Shop.

3. **Enter the following customer cheque, received on 20 June 2011:**

   Jeanette receives a cheque from Pete the Party Planner for £242.40. She pays this into the bank using payslip reference 100010, as shown in Figure 6-14.

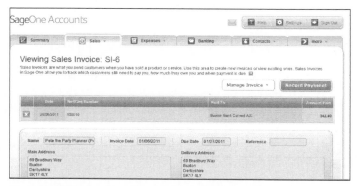

Figure 6-14: The invoice after a payment has been allocated.

4. **Enter the following payment details made to Paper Products Ltd on 2 May 2011:**

   Because money is a bit tight at the moment, Jeanette agrees with Paper Products Ltd to pay the invoice in two parts. She writes a cheque out for £150. The cheque number is 000003.

   You can check your answers to question 4 by referring back to Figures 6-9 to 6-11.

5. **Enter the payment made to Derby Wholesale Cards on 3 May 2011:**

   Jeanette receives a statement from Derby Wholesale Cards who politely remind her that she owes £140.40. Charlotte writes a cheque number 000004, to clear the debt.

   You can check that you've paid Derby Wholesale Cards correctly by running an outstanding Sales Invoice report. If the invoice isn't listed, it's no longer outstanding and you can assume that you've correctly paid it off. You can also check by viewing the invoice from the invoice list and checking the payment information that you've entered.

If you want to, you can run Outstanding Sales and Purchase Invoice reports to see what remains after entering all these transactions. If correct, they look something like Figures 6-15 and 6-16.

Figure 6-15: The outstanding sales invoices as at 30 June 2011.

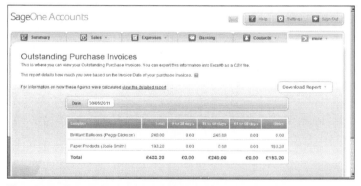

Figure 6-16: The outstanding purchase invoices as at 30 June 2011.

Chapter 7

Banking on Your Bank Accounts

● ●

In This Chapter

▶ Using the default bank accounts

▶ Logging bank receipts and payments

▶ Dealing with petty cash and credit cards

▶ Reconciling your bank account

● ●

*M*aintaining your bank accounts and moving money around efficiently are crucial aspects of running a business successfully, which makes this chapter one of the most important in the book; please don't skip it! Reading this chapter ensures that you've entered all your transactions correctly and that your future reports (such as those I describe in Chapter 9) are accurate.

In Chapter 6, I discussed how you allocate customer receipts and supplier payments to Sage One, but I didn't look at all the other types of income and expense that a business incurs on a day-to-day basis. This chapter fills in those gaps.

Counting On Your Default Bank Accounts

Sage One gives you a Current account and a Cash in Hand account as defaults when you register with Sage One.

Keeping current with your Current account

This account is usually your regular bank current account. You may also have other accounts that you need to open in Sage, including perhaps deposit accounts. Have a look at Chapter 3 for all about opening new accounts.

Handling your Cash in Hand account

This account is one of the individual features of Sage One. At first glance you may think that it's the equivalent of a petty cash account, but not so. You can find more details about using a petty cash account in the later section 'Dealing with Petty Cash'.

The Cash in Hand account is designed to be the place that you first receive your money. For example, you can see it as your back pocket, or perhaps a cheque sent to your office: it may even be cash sales from your till.

When you enter a cash sale into Sage One, it automatically deposits into the Cash in Hand account. You can then transfer this amount into your bank account, assuming that you want the money to go there. I cover this process in the 'Transferring Money between Bank Accounts' section, later in this chapter.

Editing your bank account

You may find that you need to edit your bank account details. For example, you may want to customise the name of the bank account rather than just call it Current. Here's how you can do so:

1. **Click the Banking tab.** You see that the default bank accounts appear as well as any new accounts that you've created.

2. **Click the account you want to edit.** The viewing account screen opens as shown in Figure 7-1.

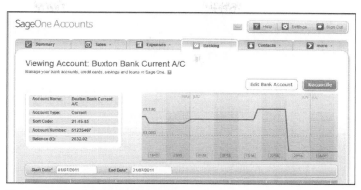

Figure 7-1: Viewing the bank account.

3. **Click Edit Bank Account.** The appropriate window opens as shown in Figure 7-2.

   You can amend the account name and add sort code and account details if they aren't already entered. You also have the option to enter the bank address and contact details if you desire.

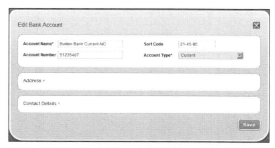

Figure 7-2: Editing the bank account details.

4. **Click Save when you're happy with the details you've entered.** A confirmation message appears saying that you've successfully saved the information. The revised bank account details now appear on the Banking screen.

Entering Other Bank Payments and Receipts

Your business doesn't only have cash sales, it also receives cash in other ways: as bank interest, dividends, loans and so on. Money received in this way is known as Other Income in Sage One, rather than Sales, because it's not generated from products that you sell.

Here's how to enter Other Income in Sage One:

1. **Hover over the Sales tab and click Other Income.** A new window called Other Income opens. Here you can record cash sales, which is particularly useful if you don't need to create sales invoices in Sage One but just want to record the cash received. You can also record any other income. The screen is split into three boxes that need completing, as shown in Figure 7-3.

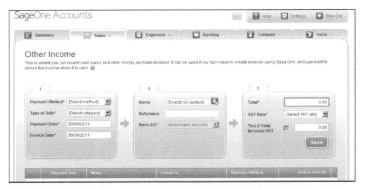

Figure 7-3: Other Income screen for entering cash sales and other income.

2. **Enter the necessary details in Box 1:**

   • **Payment method:** Choose Bank Receipt (such as a standing order), Cash Receipt (literally cash as in notes/coins) or Cheque in Hand (any cheques received).

   • **Type of Sale:** Here you can choose Bank Charges and Interest, Other Income or Sales. You can also create a new sales type by clicking Create new link at the bottom of the drop down list.

- **Payment Date:** Enter the date that the money was paid in.

- **Invoice Date:** The invoice date defaults to the payment date, and is there so that if the transaction you're posting is subject to VAT, Sage One automatically puts it on your VAT return. If you don't have an invoice date, don't worry; just let Sage give it the payment date.

The options you select in Box 1 have a direct effect on what you enter in Box 2. For example, if I were to enter that the payment method was a Bank Receipt in Box 1, Box 2 automatically defaults to my Buxton Bank Current account, because this bank account is the only one I have set up.

3. **Enter details into Box 2 as required:**

   - **Name:** You can enter a customer name here, if you want to record a cash sale against a customer without actually raising an invoice. You can also use the new contact icon to create a new customer.

   - **Reference:** If you're recording bank interest, you can make a note of the interest period.

   - **Bank Account:** Select the bank account that you want to use.

4. **Enter details into Box 3:**

   - **Total:** Enter the total amount received.

   - **VAT rate:** Select the VAT rate if applicable.

   - **Tick box:** Tick if total includes VAT.

   If you aren't VAT-registered, these boxes won't appear.

5. **Click Save when you've checked all the details you entered.** A confirmation message appears saying that the transaction was posted successfully.

You can see an example of how cash takings are entered in Figure 7-4.

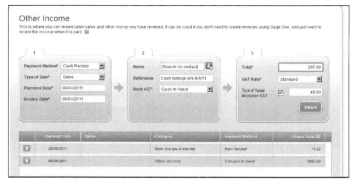

Figure 7-4: Entering cash takings into Sage One.

Recurring income

Sometimes you receive the same income time and time again. Sage One gives you the ability to enter repeating income by setting it up once and then Sage automatically repeats the transaction regularly, either daily, weekly or monthly.

To set up a recurring income entry, follow these steps:

1. **From the main screen, click Sales and select the Other Income link from the drop down menu.**

2. **Scroll down the list of existing receipts and select the one you want to repeat.**

3. **Click the repeat button and the Recurring Income window opens up, as shown in Figure 7-5.** Tell Sage how many times and how often you wish to repeat the transaction. Then click save.

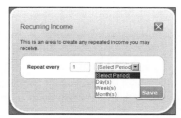

Figure 7-5: Entering recurring income.

Stopping the recurring income

All good things come to an end, and you need to know how to deal with income that suddenly stops coming in. Here's how:

1. **From the main screen, click Sales and then Other Income from the drop down menu.**

2. **Highlight the recurring receipt that you want to stop.** Notice that a new button appears on the screen called Edit Recurrence.

3. **Click the Edit Recurrence button followed by the Stop Recurrence button which subsequently appears.** A confirmation message appears saying that the recurring income entry has been successfully stopped.

Paying cheques into your bank account

As I mention earlier in the 'Handling your Cash in Hand account' section, when you enter cash sales into Sage One, the system automatically enters the cash into the Cash in Hand bank account. The same thing applies when you enter cheques into Sage One via the Other Income method. You then need to manually move this cash into the correct bank account (assuming that you've paid it all into your bank account, of course!).

The easiest way to approach this task is to use the paying in book and enter each entry from this source. That way, you correctly pick up all cash and cheques entered.

Here's how you move the money:

1. **Click the Banking button.** Your bank accounts appear.

2. **Click to select the Cash in Hand account.** The viewing account screen opens for your Cash in Hand account.

3. **You can either select the date range appropriate to the transactions you want to locate from this page or skip straight to Step 4.** Choosing a date range loads all

the transactions for the date range that you select, as shown in Figure 7-6. If you skip directly to Step 4, Sage One loads all transactions available which could be quite a few.

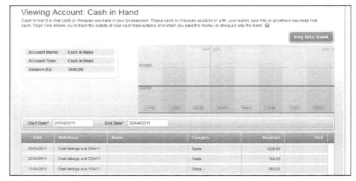

Figure 7-6: Viewing the transactions for a specific date range in the Cash in Hand account.

4. **Click the Pay into Bank button on the top right side of the screen.** A new window opens with two boxes as shown in Figure 7-7.

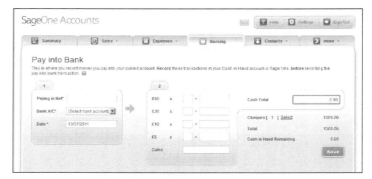

Figure 7-7: Pay into Bank screen.

5. **Enter details into Box 1:**

    • **Paying in reference:** This is the reference in your paying-in book.

- **Bank account:** Select the appropriate bank account – this usually defaults to your bank current account if no other bank account has been set up.

- **Date:** This is the date that you're paying the money into your account.

6. **Enter in Box 2 the cash and cheques that you're paying in, just as you would enter them in your paying-in book.** You don't have to allocate the cash in the same level of detail as your paying-in slip, unless of course you want to. Instead you can simply enter the total amount of cash.

   Notice in box 2 the section for cheques. You can see from Figure 7-7 that the number one in brackets is after the word Cheques and a value of £1,000 is against this, to indicate that I entered one cheque into Sage One for the sum of £1,000. (I did this through Other Income, and selected Cheque in Hand as my payment method, which is why it appears in my Cash in Hand account; Sage One automatically sends any cheques received into this account there.)

7. **Click Select link to pay in this cheque.** The Select Cheques window appears as shown in Figure 7-8. Notice that a tick is already against this cheque. You can untick any cheques shown by clicking once on the cheque you want to deselect.

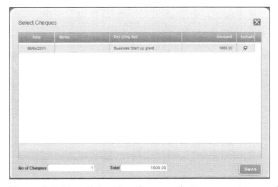

Figure 7-8: Identifying the cheques that you want to pay into your bank account.

8. **Click Save.** You're returned to the Pay into Bank screen.

9. **Check that the paying in details are correct, including the cash amount and the cheque amounts, and when you're happy, click Save.** A confirmation message appears saying that you've successfully made a new deposit. The amount that you paid in appears at the bottom of the Pay into Bank screen as shown in Figure 7-9.

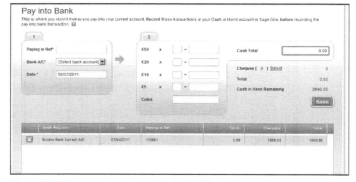

Figure 7-9: Shows the amount deposited into your bank account.

When you click to the Banking screen, you can see that your Cash in Hand account balance has been reduced by the amount that you have paid into the Current account. Likewise, you see that your bank current account balance has increased by the amount you have paid in.

Enter all your deposits to your bank in this way, using your paying-in book as a guide.

Tick the paying in slip stub to indicate that you've entered the money into Sage One. That way, you know exactly where you can start from when you next start entering some cash.

Making payments other than supplier payments

On plenty of occasions, money goes out of your bank account that isn't directly related to your suppliers, and these amounts have to be dealt with differently in Sage One.

Although lots of types of other payments exist, here are just a few examples:

- ✔ Bank interest and charges
- ✔ Loan payments
- ✔ VAT payments
- ✔ Wages bills

Here's how you enter these types of transactions:

1. **Hover over the Expenses tab and select Other Expenses from the dropdown menu.** The relevant window opens as shown in Figure 7-10. Three boxes need completing.

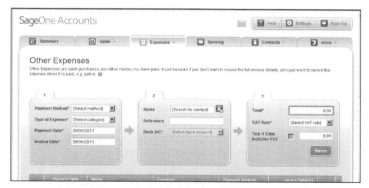

Figure 7-10: Showing the Other Expenses window.

2. **Enter details into Box 1:**
   - Choose a Payment Method: Bank Payment (such as a standing order; include here cheques that you write to people), Cash Payment (notes and coins) or Credit Card Payment.

- Select type of expense (Sage provides a long list of expense types as shown in Figure 7-11, or you can create a new expense type by selecting Create New from the dropdown menu).

- Enter the payment date.

- Enter the invoice date (if relevant, otherwise Sage automatically defaults to the payment date).

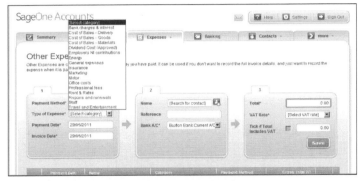

Figure 7-11: Showing the different expense types.

3. **Enter necessary details into Box 2.**

- Name of contact (if applicable). You can also use the New Contact icon to create a new supplier record here.

- A reference, such as wages for June, and also a note of the cheque number so that you can easily identify the payment on your bank reconciliation.

- The bank account (use the dropdown arrow to select the correct account).

4. **Enter details into Box 3:**

- Total amount paid.

- VAT rate if applicable, or select No VAT.

- Tick box if total includes VAT.

5. **Click Save, when you're happy that all the details are correct.** An appropriate message appears confirming that you've processed the transaction successfully.

Shelling Out with Expenses

All businesses have expenses, of course. Often they recur every month and sometimes you have to refund one. This section gives you all the necessary info.

Setting up a recurring expense

To save having to enter them every time, you can set up a recurring expense within Sage One. For example, if you have a subscription fee that comes out of your account every month, you can set up a recurring transaction for it as follows:

1. **From the main screen, click Expenses, and then Other Expenses, and scroll down the screen.** You see a list of all the existing payments that you've made.

2. **Click the expense that you want to repeat and scroll back up to the top of the screen.** You now see the details of that expense.

3. **Click the Repeat button, as shown in Figure 7-12.** The Recurring Expense window opens as shown in Figure 7-13. Enter how often you want that expense to repeat, for example, daily, weekly, monthly.

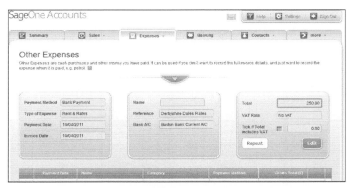

Figure 7-12: Click the repeat button to set up a recurring transaction.

Figure 7-13: Completing the recurring expense details.

4. **Click Save when you've entered the recurring expense details.** A confirmation message appears saying that the recurring transaction has been set up successfully. You can also see that two little green arrows appear next to your recurring transaction on the list of other expenses. This expense now appears every month in your bank account until you tell it to stop.

Stopping a recurring expense

If you've set up a recurring expense and now want to stop it, here's how:

1. **Click the Expenses tab and then Other Expenses and highlight the payment that you want to edit.** Notice that a new button appears on the screen called Edit Recurrence, as shown in Figure 7-14.

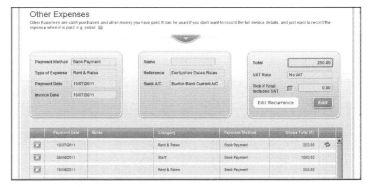

Figure 7-14: Editing a recurring entry.

2. **Click Stop Recurrence in the Recurring Expense window.** Then click Save.

The recurring expense has now stopped.

Refunding expenses

Sometimes you need to refund an expense that previously came out of your account. Sage One allows you to do so, as follows:

1. **From the main screen, click the Expenses tab and then Other Expenses.**

2. **Enter the payment method as a Bank Payment and type the necessary dates.**

3. **Add a useful reference in the field, such as 'refund on rates', as shown in Figure 7-15.**

4. **Ensure that you select the correct bank account in box 2.**

5. **Enter the amount as a negative amount in box 3 and tick the appropriate VAT boxes.**

6. **Click Save when you're happy with the details.**

A confirmation message appears saying that the transaction has been successfully completed.

Figure 7-15: Entering a refund on expenses.

Transferring Money between Bank Accounts

You may sometimes need to move money between your bank accounts. For example, perhaps you want to create a petty cash float and transfer some funds into that, or you need to pay your monthly credit card bill. You can do all these tasks via a bank transfer:

1. **Click the Banking tab.** Hover over the Manage Bank Accounts button and then click Transfer from the dropdown menu. A new window opens, as shown in Figure 7-16.

Figure 7-16: The transfer window.

2. **Using the dropdown arrows, select the accounts that you want to transfer to and from.** For example, if you want to pay your credit card bill, you'd transfer money from your Current account to your Credit Card account.

   You can also pay yourself drawings from the business in this way. For example, the 'from' account would be the business account, and the 'to' account would be Drawings. The flip side is if you decide to invest some money into the business. The 'from' account would be Capital Investment and the 'to' account would be the business current account.

3. **Click Save, when you're happy with the transfer details.** A confirmation message appears saying that your transfer has been made successfully.

Getting Petty: Dealing with Petty Cash

In any business, small amounts have to be paid out in cash, ranging from tea and coffee, stamps or even payments to the window cleaner! Most businesses keep a petty cash tin, which holds a small amount of money for these items.

The easiest way to deal with petty cash in Sage One is to create a new bank account called Petty Cash. You can transfer some money from the bank Current account into the Petty Cash account to give it a float to start with (as I describe in the preceding section).

You can use what's called an *Imprest system,* which basically means that you can reconcile the petty cash float by adding the total amount of receipts to the total amount of cash left in the tin, and this should equal the total amount of the float. If it doesn't balance, usually someone has taken money out of the tin and not put a receipt back in the tin.

To make a payment from your Petty Cash account, follow the instructions for the earlier section 'Making payments other than supplier payments' and select Bank Payments. This payment isn't considered a cash payment here, because I recommend that you set up Petty Cash as a separate bank account. If you ensure that the account type is Current, it appears on your dropdown list of bank accounts in box 2. See Figure 7-17 for an example of stamps being purchased from Petty Cash.

Figure 7-17: Making a payment from the Petty Cash account.

Carrying on with Credit Cards

Lots of businesses find that credit cards are very useful as long as the spending is carefully controlled. Most business credit cards are paid off in full at the end of each month, which makes reconciling a bit easier. You can, however, get quite a shock at the end of the month when you have to find a chunk of cash to pay the credit card bill.

Keep all your receipts, because they can be used to claim back VAT (if you're VAT registered) and they make reconciling the credit card statement much easier.

You reconcile credit card statements in exactly the same way as a bank statement, but you enter the figure as a negative amount because it's money that you owe (check out the later section 'Reconciling Your Bank Account' for more details.

Processing a payment on your credit card

When you receive your credit card statement, processing the payments is really easy.

Make sure that you have all the receipts attached to the credit card statement, so that you can see the VAT element of each transaction. Even if you're not VAT registered, being able to check your credit card statement against actual receipts is still useful.

Then:

1. **Click the Expenses tab.** Select Other Expenses from the dropdown menu.

2. **Enter details for Box 1:**

   - Select the payment method as Credit Card Payment, which automatically adjusts the bank account in box 2 to be your Credit Card account.

   - Use the dropdown menu to select the type of expense.

   - Enter the payment date and the invoice date.

3. **Enter details for Box 2:**

   - Enter a reference – such as the supplier's name.

   - Using the dropdown arrow, select the appropriate credit card, if you have more than one.

4. **Enter details for Box 3:**

   - Enter the total amount.

   - Using the dropdown arrow, select the appropriate VAT rate.

   - Tick the box if the amount you entered includes VAT.

5. **Click Save when you've checked all the details and are happy that they're correct.** A confirmation message appears on the screen saying that the transaction has been successful.

Figure 7-18 shows some stationery being purchased by credit card.

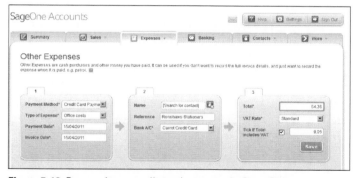

Figure 7-18: Processing a credit card payment in Sage One.

Making a payment against your credit card

As well as finding the items of expenditure on your credit card statement, you also find details of amounts paid off against the card. Normally you pay a credit card via a direct debit from your bank account, and so the easiest way to process that payment is via a bank transfer.

For how to do so, check out the earlier section 'Transferring Money between Bank Accounts'.

Settling Any Differences: Reconciling Your Bank Account

Bank reconciliation is where you check that the bank payments and receipts within Sage One match the transactions on your bank statements for the same period.

No doubt some differences exist to begin with, such as bank interest or charges that you haven't accounted for in Sage. The process of bank reconciliation allows you to highlight those differences and post the necessary bank transactions into Sage.

To perform a bank reconciliation within Sage One, follow these steps:

1. **Click the Banking tab and select the bank account you want to reconcile.** Doing so opens up the Viewing Account page.

2. **Click the Reconcile button (at the top right of the screen).**The Getting Started window appears (see Figure 7-19), where you need to enter the statement date and balance and any reference you want to use.

SageOne Accounts

Summary | Sales | Expenses | Banking | Contacts | more

Reconcile: Buxton Bank Current A/C

The Bank Reconciliation process helps you make sure your financial data is correct by allowing you to match figures in Sage One against those shown on your bank statement.

Get Started | Match | Summary

Start the reconciliation process by entering information from your bank statement to tell Sage One what it is trying to match up to.

Enter the statement end date*   30/04/2011

Enter the statement end balance*   2510.55

Enter the statement reference   April 2011 Ban Rec

Figure 7-19: Getting started with your bank reconciliation.

3. **Click Next.** A list of transactions appears with a tick box next to them, as shown in Figure 7-20. If the item appears on your bank statement, tick the item on the screen and also on your statement.

   The totals change in the matched section to the right of the screen. Ensure that the difference is zero before proceeding to the next screen.

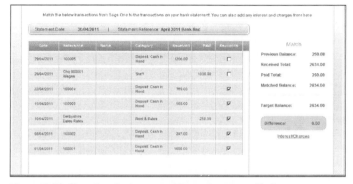

Figure 7-20: Showing the items waiting to be reconciled.

4. **Click Next when you're happy with the details.** You're taken to a match screen, as shown in Figure 7-21, which is confirmation of what you've matched so far.

5. **Click Save when you're satisfied.** A confirmation message appears saying that you've reconciled the account successfully.

Figure 7-21: The final part of the bank reconciliation.

Trying Things Yourself

Here's your opportunity to practise the tasks that I describe in this chapter.

1. **6 April 2011: Jeanette receives a business start up grant of £1,000, to cover purchasing stock and setting up the shop.** She banks the cheque using Payslip 100001. Enter this amount, treating it as Other Income (as I describe in the earlier section 'Entering Other Bank Receipts').

2. **Enter the following cash takings from the till for the stated weeks.**

   You need to use the Other Income screen to enter this cash.

   - 8 April 2011: £297: Payslip ref 100002
   - 15 April 2011: £568: Payslip ref 100003
   - 22 April 2011: £769: Payslip ref 100004
   - 29 April 2011: £1,206: Payslip ref 100005

   Make sure that you then Pay into Bank the above amounts so that they appear in your bank current account when you come to reconcile it.

3. **Enter the following payments:**

   - 10 April 2011: Derbyshire Dales rates £250 (paid via direct debit).

     This amount needs to be paid as Other Expenses and Bank Payment selected as the Payment Method. That way, it can be allocated directly to the bank account and should be picked up easily in the bank reconciliation.

   - 29 April 2011: Cheque 00001 for wages £1,000.

   Again, select the Other Expenses method because there's not going to be an invoice for this item. Again, select Bank Payment as your payment method.

4. **Reconcile the bank account as at 31 May 2011.**

   You should have two entries that you can't reconcile:

   - Cheque 000001 wages £1,000
   - Cash Payslip 1000005 £1,206

These payments haven't yet cleared the bank and are therefore unpresented at the month-end.

5. **Reconcile the Credit Card account as at 31 May 2011.**

6. **Create a Petty Cash account (see Chapter 3 for how to set up a bank account) and then transfer £150 from the Bank Current account to the Petty Cash account on 20 May 2011.**

   Make the following payments out of the Petty Cash account:

   6a. Stamps: £2.46

   6b. Window cleaner: £20.00

Use account type Current when you set up your Petty Cash account. That way, you can make your payment method a bank payment and you're able to select the Petty Cash account.

Answering Trying Things Yourself

Here are the answers to the previous questions.

1. **Figure 7-22 shows you the best way to enter a business grant.**

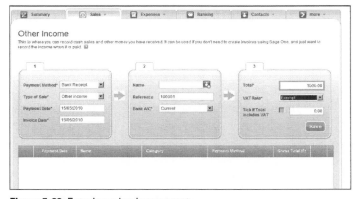

Figure 7-22: Entering a business grant.

2. Check Figure 7-4 to see how to record cash takings and Figure 7-9 for how to Pay into Bank.

3. Figure 7-23 shows how to enter the Derbyshire Dales rates bill.

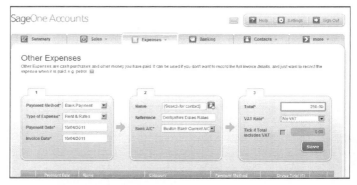

Figure 7-23: Entering a rates payment.

Figure 7-24 shows how the wages payment should be made

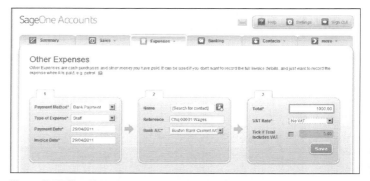

Figure 7-24: Entering a wages payment.

4. Refer to Figure 7-20 to see the items that haven't been reconciled and remain unpresented on the bank reconciliation.

5. Take a look at Figure 7-25 to see an example of a reconciled credit card.

Figure 7-25: A reconciled credit card.

6. **Figure 7-26 shows you how to transfer funds to a Petty Cash account.**

Figure 7-26: Transferring funds to a Petty Cash account.

6a. **Figure 7-17 shows you how to make a petty cash payment for stamps.**

6b. **Figure 7-27 shows you how to pay your window cleaner from Petty Cash.**

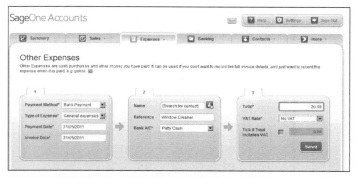

Figure 7-27: Paying your window cleaner by petty cash.

Chapter 8

Running Your VAT Return

In This Chapter

▶ Setting up your VAT return

▶ Sending your VAT return to HMRC

▶ Paying your VAT

▶ Getting in some VAT practice

*I*n this chapter, I describe how to use Sage One to get your VAT facts exact (VAT as in value-added tax, of course, and nothing to do with storing wine!).

This chapter is applicable only if you're VAT registered. The rest of you can quite happily ignore this one! If you're unsure about whether you need to register, check out the nearby sidebar 'Becoming VAT registered or not'.

As I mention in Chapter 2, Sage One supports several VAT schemes:

✔ Standard VAT (currently at 20 per cent)

✔ Flat rate invoice based

✔ Flat rate cash based

✔ VAT cash accounting

For more details on any of the above schemes, visit the HMRC (Her Majesty's Revenue and Customs) website at www.hmrc.gov.uk. Also, flip to Chapter 2 for a brief overview of these schemes.

Download the definitive guide to all things VAT-related – Notice 700: The VAT Guide.

Becoming VAT registered or not

To know whether you have to register your business for VAT, you need to be aware of the VAT registration threshold. This is the amount of VAT taxable turnover your business can reach before you need to register for VAT. At present, the current VAT registration threshold is £73,000, but this amount changes every year in the Budget and so regularly check your turnover to see if you're under or over the threshold.

You can voluntarily register if you want to claim back VAT even when your turnover is less than the threshold.

Visit www.hmrc.gov.uk for further information: the website contains a range of useful articles regarding VAT and whether you need to register.

Creating a VAT Return

Generating a VAT return in Sage One is very easy, just follow the instructions below. Ensure that you check the information before you submit it!

1. **Starting from the main screen, hover over the More tab, and select VAT Returns from the dropdown list.** The VAT submissions screen opens.

2. **Click the Create Report for HMRC button, to start the VAT Return Wizard.** See Figure 8-1.

Figure 8-1: Starting the VAT Return Wizard.

3. **Check that a tick appears in the Create VAT Return box, and then click Next to continue.** The second page of the VAT Wizard opens as shown in Figure 8-2.

Figure 8-2: Entering the VAT return dates.

4. **Select the period for the VAT return.** This is usually a quarterly period, but can be monthly depending on your arrangements with HMRC. Note: You can edit this information in your Financial Settings area, should you need to amend it.

5. **Check your entries.** When happy, tick the box to confirm that you've entered all the transactions for the relevant VAT period.

6. **Click Next to continue.** A summary VAT return appears, as shown in Figure 8-3.

Figure 8-3: Viewing the VAT summary.

You can adjust the figures if you feel that they're incorrect. If you click the Print button, you get a VAT summary in PDF format, as shown in Figure 8-4.

VAT Report (Summary)

Include prior transactions:No

From Date: 01/04/2011   To Date: 30/06/2011

VAT due in this period on Sales	1	541.66
VAT due in this period on EC acquisitions	2	0.00
Total VAT due (sum of boxes 1 and 2)	3	541.66
VAT reclaimed in this period on purchases	4	49.06
Net VAT to be paid to HMRC or reclaimed by you	5	492.60
Total value of sales, excluding VAT	6	3708.26
Total value of purchases, excluding VAT	7	247.76
Total value of EC sales, excluding VAT	8	0.00
Total value of EC purchases, excluding VAT	9	0.00

Figure 8-4: Showing the VAT summary in PDF format.

You also have the opportunity to print a detailed VAT report, which shows the individual transactions that make up the VAT return.

7. **Click Next when you're happy with the figures.** The final screen of the wizard appears (see Figure 8-5). You can submit the VAT return direct through Sage One or online via HMRC's website (as I describe in the next section 'Submitting Your VAT Return').

After creating your VAT return, you need to check it to make sure that you're not submitting a load of rubbish information!

The easiest way is to print a report as mentioned above in Step 6, which provides you with a list of all invoices and transactions that make up your current VAT return. You can ensure that you've included all your invoices by checking back to your sales invoice file, or checking that no gaps exist in the sequential numbering system.

Figure 8-5: Submitting your VAT return – choosing your option.

Submitting Your VAT Return

You can submit your VAT return to HMRC in one of two ways: directly through Sage One or online through the HMRC website (taking the information from your Sage One reports). For both methods, you need to register with HMRC, as I describe in the following section.

Registering to submit your VAT returns online

To submit your VAT returns online, you need to register with HMRC first. The process is relatively easy but does take a few days to set up, and so allow yourself plenty of time.

To sign up for the service go to www.hmrc.gov.uk. From the Do it Online section on the left, click the Register (new users) link and follow the instructions on the screen, as shown in Figure 8-6.

Figure 8-6: Registering for HMRC online services.

During the above registration process, you're issued with a User ID. Make a note of this and keep it safe, because you need it every time you log in to HMRC online services.

An activation code is sent to your principal place of business by post, and this letter can take between 7–10 days to arrive. The envelope is marked Government Gateway. You need to activate your online service within 28 days of receiving the activation code, otherwise it expires and you have to apply for another one.

Provide HMRC with your email address, so that they can send you a reminder when your VAT return is due. This reminder can be really useful, because when you get stuck into the thick of business, the last thing you're apt to remember is when your return's due!

Using HMRC's website

Ensure that you've signed up for the VAT online service, as I outline in the preceding section. When HMRC has sent you the Government Gateway User ID, follow these steps to submit your VAT return online:

1. **Go to HMRC's website** www.hmrc.gov.uk **and click the Log In link from the Do It Online section on the left side of the website.** The Welcome to Online Services screen opens as shown in Figure 8-7.

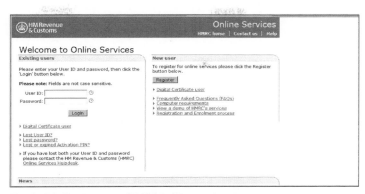

Figure 8-7: Signing on to HMRC online services.

2. **Provide your User ID and password as requested.** You're then taken to Your HMRC services page. Here, you can select the service that you want to use – in this case submit your VAT return.

3. **Select the link to Submit a Return/Set Up a VAT Direct Debit Instruction' or 'Access Service' to the right side of the screen.** The appropriate screen opens to allow you to select the period for which you want to submit a return. Only outstanding returns appear on this list, and so there should be only one!

4. **Fill in the boxes on the screen as you would on paper.** You can use Sage One's generated reports to help you.

5. **Check and make sure that the details you've entered match those of the Sage reports.** You can't amend the return online after you submit it, so make sure that you check it thoroughly.

   If you want, you can save a draft return and come back to it later.

6. **Click Next and you're taken to the VAT Submission page.** You're asked to re-enter your User ID and password for security purposes.

7. **Click Submit and your return is sent automatically to HMRC.** You should receive an Acknowledgement page, which confirms that the VAT return has been submitted successfully.

I usually print this out and keep it on file with my VAT returns, just in case any problems arise later and I need to prove that I sent the return.

So that's it – you're done!

Sending your return directly from Sage One

From the submission page of the VAT Wizard (see the earlier Figure 8-5), you can click the Submit online with Sage One button and the following screen opens (check out Figure 8-8).

Figure 8-8: Submitting your VAT return via Sage One.

Enter your Government Gateway User ID and password, which is sent to you when you register to use the online HMRC submission service. Then follow the online screen instructions to complete your VAT submission. The VAT Submissions list then displays a status of Manual Submission, Pending, Online or Failed.

Print out copies of the submission confirmation for your records and file them with your VAT return.

Coughing Up: Paying VAT

The preceding sections give you all the details on creating and submitting your VAT return, but of course you also have to pay the VAT!

Once the VAT return is saved, Sage One automatically posts transactions for the VAT liability. For example, if you owe HMRC some money, Sage One creates a purchase invoice to reflect the liability. On the other hand, if (in the rare instance), HMRC owes you money, Sage One creates a sales invoice to reflect the amount owed.

These invoices are then paid through the normal payment of invoice process as outlined in Chapter 6.

If you file your VAT electronically, you must also pay your VAT electronically.

Electronic payment methods include:

- ✔ Internet banking.
- ✔ Telephone banking.
- ✔ Debit or credit card via the Internet using Billpay.
- ✔ BACS direct credit (usually free).
- ✔ CHAPs (usually a charge).
- ✔ Direct debit (see www.hmrc.gov.uk/payinghmrc/ vat.htm for how to set up a direct debit).
- ✔ Bank Giro Credit transfer (you can pay by cash or cheque at a bank supporting this facility; you can't use the Post Office counter).

For all the above methods you need the HMRC bank account details, which you can find by clicking on the link in the direct debit section of the website.

The benefit of paying electronically is that you often have a little longer to pay. For example, if your VAT period ends 30 June 2011, your VAT return is due on 31 July 2011; however, you have until 7 August to pay the VAT. This extra time can make all the difference from a cash flow point of view.

One of the safest and most convenient ways to pay is via direct debit. Setting this process up is very simple and you only need to do it once. When your direct debit is set up, HMRC collects only the amount that you declare on your VAT return.

You need to allow at least five working days after setting up a direct debit before filing your first return online. If you haven't allowed enough time, you have to use another electronic method.

Having a Go Yourself

Now is your chance to run the Jingles VAT return for the period 1 April 2011–30 June 2011.

Follow steps 1–6 as I describe in the earlier section 'Creating a VAT Return'. Click the Print button when you reach stage 3 of the VAT Wizard, and then compare your results to those shown in Figure 8-4 shown earlier in this chapter.

Don't worry if the data in your reports doesn't look exactly the same as mine. I added some more transactions into my dataset to create more interest to the screenshots.

Chapter 9

Preparing Reports

● ●

In This Chapter

▶ Deciding which reports to use

▶ Producing your reports

▶ Knowing who may want these reports, and why

● ●

*Y*ou need to obtain and check regular accounts reports in order to successfully monitor the financial situation of your business. You can't take prompt and accurate decisions without the right up-to-date information. Sage One allows you to prepare and produce a range of reports. Although the list isn't extensive, you have access to the usual management reports such as Profit and Loss and Balance Sheet, as well as the Trial Balance, Outstanding Sales and Purchase Invoice reports.

In this chapter, I describe producing these reports and who finds the information useful.

Looking at the Reports Sage One Can Run

Here's how to peruse and access the reports Sage One can produce for you. You can access them from the main screen, using the More tab.

1. **Hover over the More tab and then click Reports.** The reports window opens as shown in Figure 9-1.

   As you can see, the following reports are available:

   • Profit and Loss report

   • Balance Sheet report

- Outstanding Sales Invoice report (check out Chapter 6, Figures 6-4 and 6-5 for how to produce this report).

- Outstanding Purchase Invoice report (again, flip to Chapter 6 and Figure 6-12 for more details)

- Trial Balance

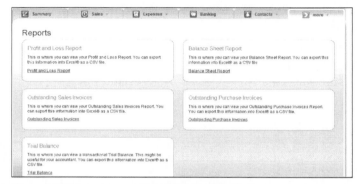

Figure 9-1: The reports you can select on Sage One.

2. **Select the report you want to open by clicking on the link specific to that report.**

3. **Enter the date required to run the report you want.**

4. **Hover over the Download the Report button – you have the option to print a PDF file or export to a CSV (comma separated values) file.** The latter allows you to export the data into a spreadsheet or other software such as a database. You can then adapt the information to suit.

Using the Different Reports

In this section, I examine each available report in turn, explaining why you may want to run it and who's going to find it useful. Remember that I deal with producing Outstanding Sales Invoice and Outstanding Purchase Invoice reports in Chapter 6.

Checking your Profit and Loss report

This report shows whether your business made a profit or a loss for the period selected.

The report starts by showing you the sales revenue for the business and breaks it down in the component parts. For example in Figure 9-2, you can see that in the Sales category, the report shows Other Income as well as Sales.

Sage One deducts Direct Expenses from Sales Revenue to find the Gross Profit for the business. Finally, the software deducts the overheads to find the Net Profit.

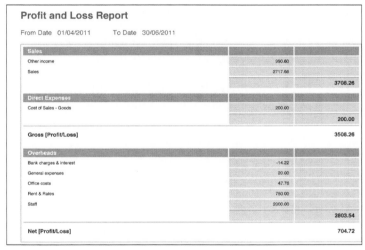

Profit and Loss Report

From Date 01/04/2011   To Date 30/06/2011

Sales		
Other income	990.60	
Sales	2717.66	
		3708.26

Direct Expenses		
Cost of Sales - Goods	200.00	
		200.00

| Gross [Profit/Loss] | | 3508.26 |

Overheads		
Bank charges & interest	-14.22	
General expenses	20.00	
Office costs	47.76	
Rent & Rates	750.00	
Staff	2000.00	
		2803.54

| Net [Profit/Loss] | | 704.72 |

Figure 9-2: An example of the Profit and Loss report.

This report is useful for the owner/manager of a business because it provides a benchmark for how well the business is performing. If you run the report month by month, you start to see trends developing over time. For example, your business may be cyclical and the Profit and Loss reflects this fact, perhaps by showing a dip in sales figures during certain times of the year.

You can calculate a gross profit percentage by dividing the gross profit by the total sales figure and so compare this figure to the industry standard benchmarks. Doing so gives you a good indication as to whether your business is performing as well as it should (or could) be.

Your accountant uses this report when calculating your tax computations at the end of each fiscal year, and so it serves many purposes.

Running a Balance Sheet report

The balance sheet is a snapshot of a business's finances at a particular point in time. Most people choose to run a Balance Sheet report at the month- and year-end as part of their usual accounting routines.

This report shows a list of assets and liabilities and the sources of funds that have helped finance the business. Have a look at Figure 9-3 to see Jingle's balance sheet.

From the balance sheet, you can see how much money is owed to the business and how much the business owes to other people.

Your accountant is likely to use this report to gauge the financial health of your business. He checks to see that the business has more assets than liabilities and therefore is in a healthy, sustainable state.

The balance sheet is also of interest to your bank manager, who can see at a glance whether your business is in tip-top financial condition.

In addition, if you're considering expanding your operations, you can use this report to assess the viability of obtaining further finance.

Balance Sheet Report

Date 30/06/2011

Fixed Assets		
		0.00

Current Assets		
Cash at Bank	2132.02	
Petty Cash	127.54	
Sales invoices not paid	177.77	
		2437.33

Total Assets		2437.33

Liabilities		
Purchase invoices not paid	433.20	
Carrot Credit Card	54.36	
VAT	430.25	
Total Liabilities		917.81

Net Assets		1519.52

Equity		
Owner Investment	1000.00	
Profit & Loss/Opening Balances	519.52	
Total Equity		1519.52

Figure 9-3: An example of a balance sheet.

Balancing things up with a Trial Balance

This report is basically a list of all your accounts within Sage One where you've posted a transaction.

As Sage One operates using a double-entry system (that is, a debit exists for every corresponding credit so that the books balance), you see a list of debit balances and credit balances. Both the column totals equal each other, which proves that your books are in balance.

You don't need to worry about balancing the books because Sage One does all that for you! See Figure 9-4 for an example of this report.

Trial Balance

From Date 01/04/2011   To Date 30/06/2011

Name	Debits	Credits
Sales Invoices not paid	86.27	
Cash at Bank	1862.02	
Purchase invoices not paid	50.40	
VAT on Sales		541.86
VAT on Purchases	49.06	
Owner Investment		1000.00
Sales		2717.66
Other income		990.60
Cost of Sales - Goods	200.00	
Staff	2000.00	
Rent & Rates	750.00	
Office costs	47.76	
Bank charges & interest		14.22
General expenses	20.00	
Carrot Credit Card	69.09	
Petty Cash	127.54	
TOTAL	**5264.14**	**5264.14**

Figure 9-4: Jingles' Trial Balance.

Your accountant is probably the main person who uses this report. He can use the numbers to enter the figures into tax computation software or accounts production software.

When you're transferring from one accounting system to another, you take your opening balances (a process I describe in Chapter 4) from this report.

Drilling down to the detail

Once you've downloaded the reports, you may want to analyse the detail.

Some figures may require a fuller explanation. Sage One makes this very simple, by giving you the option to drill down to the next level of information and discover how the numbers are calculated.

For example, say I run the Profit and Loss report as shown in steps 1 and 2 of 'Looking at the Reports Sage One Can Run' and I want to query the Other Income figure. By clicking on the figure, a new window opens, as shown in Figure 9-5, which shows the account activity for, in this case, Other Income.

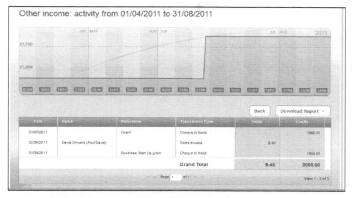

Figure 9-5: Showing the detail of Other Income.

The screen is in two parts, with a graphical illustration of the account activity at the top of the page, followed by the individual transactions listed in date order shown below. You can print out the transaction details by hovering over the Download Report button and selecting either Printable PDF or Export to CSV file.

I show you an example of a printable PDF report in Figure 9-6. This shows the breakdown of the Other Income figure from the Profit and Loss report.

Other income: activity from 01/04/2011 to 31/08/2011

Date	Name	Reference	Transaction Type	Debit	Credit
01/07/2011		Grant	Cheque In Hand		1000.00
25/06/2011	Davis Dinners (Paul Davis)		Sales Invoice	9.40	
01/04/2011		Business Start Up grant	Cheque In Hand		1000.00
			Grand Total	9.40	2000.00

Figure 9-6: Demonstrating a printable PDF of Other Income.

Reporting Yourself!

Try some of the reports for yourself. If you've been putting your transactions in as I describe in Chapters 4 to 7, you have some data that Sage can use to create reports for you.

Go ahead and have a play!

You can compare your results to Figures 9-1 to 9-6 from earlier in this chapter.

Part III
Introducing Sage One Cashbook

'There – we've got to stop storing petty cash
in a tin and use a computerised system.'

In this part . . .

I show you how you can use the Sage One Cashbook to easily manage your cashflow in and out of the business. I also show you some useful reports that you can run to assist you in running your business.

Chapter 10

Setting Up Your Sage One Cashbook

*J*ust as Elvis is king to rock'n'roll fans, cash is king to business owners. After all, cash flow is what enables your business to survive even in the most difficult times. Tracking your cash is therefore essential, which is where the Sage One Cashbook service – which I describe in this chapter and the next – comes in.

The Cashbook is accounting in its most simple format, specifically designed for sole traders operating cash-based businesses. Essentially, the system helps you to analyse your income and expenditure and (I hope!) ensure that your cash flow is positive at the end of the month.

Although Sage One Cashbook is an entirely separate service from Sage One Accounts, they share some common parts as follows:

   ✓ Setting up new bank accounts

   ✓ Setting up new customers

When the instructions for carrying out tasks in Sage One Cashbook are the same as in Sage One Accounts, I refer you to the appropriate chapter.

Understanding What Sage One Cashbook Can Do for You

The Sage One Cashbook provides a simple cash-management system, ideally suited to sole traders who operate a cash-based business. The emphasis is on *simple.*

Sage did a great deal of market research to understand the needs of such small businesses. The resulting feedback indicated that the system had to be simple to use. Business people want to spend time developing their businesses, not doing paperwork – it's the least enjoyable part of running a business (for most people!)

Therefore, this system helps you to manage your money easily and become more organised with your financial affairs, which can only be a good thing when dealing with HMRC and the bank manager!

Working with your accountant

The Cashbook is also a huge help when working with your accountant. How many times have you sent a carrier bag full of receipts to your accountant and expected her to sort through the bits of paper and provide you with a set of accounts as well as a hefty bill!

This system allows you to take ownership of your finances, and although your accountant is still available to assist you with your tax affairs and accounts, you can take control of your day-to-day activities. Your accountant can then access your records (using the Sage One Accountant Edition – see Chapter 13) as and when you're ready, or whenever you need advice on something that involves passing on your records.

The fact that your accountant can view your records without even leaving the office means that you receive an even more efficient service, because no driving time to and from your place of work is necessary. And because time is money . . . well, you can see where I'm going with this one.

If you want your accountant to use Sage One Cashbook with you, ask her to ring 0845-111-1111. Sage is happy to talk through the Sage One set-up process.

Inviting your accountant to join in the fun

If your accountant also uses Sage One, after you're registered and set up you can invite her to view your accounts through the Service Settings area, as shown in Figure 10-1.

Figure 10-1: Inviting your accountant.

Sage One sends an email to your accountant asking her to accept an invitation from you to manage the accounts via Sage One. The process is all done via messages sent online through Sage One.

After accepting the invitation, your accountant has full access to your records.

Downloading Your Free Trial

As with Sage One Accounts, you can download a free 30-day trial of the Cashbook, which allows you to test drive the software to see whether you like it.

The download process is very simple and quick. Log on to www.sageone.com and click the Cashbook window in the middle of the screen. You then see a button, 'Sign up for a free trial', as shown in Figure 10-2. Click this button and follow the wizard, which guides you step by step through signing up.

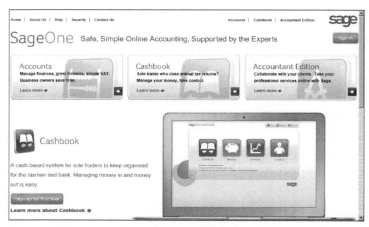

Figure 10-2: Signing up for the free trial.

The sign up process is in three parts:

1. **Enter your contact details, such as your name and address.**

   You can provide only limited information at this stage but you have the opportunity to provide more complete data when you've registered (within the Settings facility of the Cashbook).

2. **Provide some Business details.**

   These details aren't as scary as they seem. You simply need to supply what type of business you run (for example, small business or sole trader) and then input your year-end date. You also need to tick the relevant box to confirm whether you're VAT registered or not. If you are, the system asks you what VAT scheme you operate. The options are standard VAT, flat rate VAT or cash accounting.

3. **Enter some sign-in details.**

   These items consist of choosing some security questions and a password.

Tracking Your Cash with Sage One Cashbook

Nothing's more reassuring (and useful) than keeping your finger on your business's cash flow, which the Cashbook allows you to do easily and conveniently.

When you open Sage One Cashbook, after you register (see the preceding section), you're directed to the Homepage as shown in Figure 10-3. Here you're presented with four icons:

- ✔ Cashbook
- ✔ Banking
- ✔ Summary
- ✔ Contacts

Figure 10-3: The Sage One Cashbook Home screen.

In this section, I explore each of these screens in turn.

Keeping up-to-date with Cashbook

The cashbook is where you record the flow of money into and out of your business.

When you initially click the Cashbook icon you see the screen shown in Figure 10-4.

Figure 10-4: Where you record cashbook expenses.

Notice the two tabs: one called Transactions and the other Totals. The system automatically defaults to the Transactions tab.

You can toggle between the Income and the Expenses screen by clicking the circle in the top left (at first the screen is switched to the Expenses screen):

✔ The Transactions screen (whether Income or Expenses) allows you to enter your credit card transactions, as well as your BACs, direct debits, standing orders and cash transactions.

✔ The Totals tab provides a summary of all the information that you've input as shown in Figure 10-5. Obviously to start with, no transactions exist and so this looks a little boring!

Figure 10-5: Looking at the Totals tab.

Check out Chapter 11 to see how the transactions are entered and view some screenshots with information entered.

Make sure that you enter any opening balances that you may have prior to entering new data into Sage One Cashbook. For example, you may have an opening bank balance that you need to enter. Getting your opening balance right ensures that you can correctly balance your bank account at the end of each period. I demonstrate how to enter opening balances in Chapter 11.

Taking a peek at the Banking screen

This screen is where you manage all your bank accounts, cash accounts, credit cards and loan accounts. Here you can create new accounts and delete ones that you no longer need (provided that no transactions exist on the account).

Notice the Manage your Bank account button in the top right corner (shown in Figure 10-6). If you click the dropdown arrows you can see options for transferring money and creating new bank accounts. You can use the transfer option to move money from your Current account to a Petty Cash tin.

Figure 10-6: Managing your bank accounts.

Chapter 7 has all the details on how to transfer money between bank accounts.

Checking out your Summary

When you click the Summary icon, the Summary screen opens (surprise, surprise!), as shown in Figure 10-7. The screen shows a graphical representation of the funds in your bank account. The graph displays the current balance and also the movement of the bank balance throughout the month.

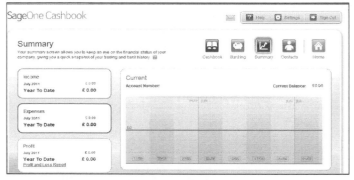

Figure 10-7: Viewing a summary of your data.

Also on the left side of the screen, you see the following:

✔ Income – for the current month and the year to date.

✔ Expenses – for the current month and the year to date.

✔ Profit – for the current month and the year to date.

You can print out a Profit and Loss report, using the link on this screen.

The Profit and Loss report is very useful, because you can see whether you're making any money or not! Obviously, all businesses want Income to be more than Expenses, but this report is one way of keeping track on a monthly basis.

Cultivating your Contacts

The Contacts icon allows you to create and manage records for the people with whom you do business, as shown in Figure 10-8.

You can set up names and addresses and telephone details, including any notes that you may want to enter, such as the best time to call them.

Figure 10-8: Setting up your Contacts.

The process for setting up your customer and supplier contacts is the same as you use for Sage One Accounts Contacts, which I describe in Chapter 3.

Checking Your Settings

You can access the Settings screen from anywhere in Sage One Cashbook. You always find it in the top right corner in between the options for Help and Sign Out.

When you click Settings, the Settings Overview screen opens as shown in Figure 10-9. The screen is split into two parts:

- My Sage One
- Sage One Cashbook

Figure 10-9: The Settings Overview screen.

The Settings section is almost exactly the same as for Sage One Accounts, so take a gander at Chapter 2 for more details. Just bear in mind that where Chapter 2 refers to Sage One Accounts, you can read Sage One Cashbook.

The one exception to the Sage One Cashbook is that it doesn't have an Invoice Settings function, because Sage One Cashbook assumes that you're a purely cash-based business and aren't going to be generating sales invoices.

Chapter 11

Entering Data into Your Cashbook

In This Chapter

▶ Keeping track of deposits with Cashbook

▶ Recording your expenses

▶ Checking whether you're making any money

*I*n Chapter 10, you discover how to navigate your way around Sage One Cashbook. I hope that reading that chapter has you champing at the bit to begin adding your business data.

In this chapter, I look at how you enter your income and expenses into the Cashbook and how to work out whether you're making as much money as you expect (note that I don't say *as much as you want!*).

You carry out many of the Cashbook tasks in the same way as with Sage One Accounts, and so where necessary I refer you to Chapter 7, instead of unnecessarily repeating myself.

Of course, the screenshots in Chapter 7 relate to Accounts rather than Cashbook, but other than that they're the same. I point out any differences.

For the purposes of demonstrating the Cashbook, in this chapter I use a fictional playgroup called Tots 'n' Toddlers. I use a different fictional company from Jingles because the Cashbook doesn't provide the additional elements of invoicing and VAT return preparation that a company like Jingles needs, but is more than adequate for a small playgroup that only needs to analyse its income and expenses. You can try out using the Cashbook yourself in the later Have a Go section 'Rehearsing using Sage One Cashbook'.

Getting Started with Opening Balances

As with any new financial system, first you need to check whether you have any opening balances to enter. (I examine this task for Sage One Accounts in Chapter 4.) The Cashbook is no different, except that you only input bank account balances and not sales or purchase invoices into this more simple system.

To access the opening balances screen, you need to do the following:

1. **Click Settings and then Financial Settings.** On this screen you can view the financial year-end date and what VAT scheme you're operating, as shown in Figure 11-1. In this case, you can see that Tots 'n' Toddlers isn't VAT registered.

Figure 11-1: Checking the Financial Settings.

2. **Click the Opening Balances link from the Financial Settings pages.** The Opening Balances wizard opens as shown in Figure 11-2.

3. **Enter the start date for your opening balances.** I use
   31 March 2011 because that's the closing date of the
   prior year, and so creates the opening position for
   April 2011.

Figure 11-2: Viewing the Opening Balances wizard.

4. **Click Next, and the second page of the wizard opens
   (see Figure 11-3).** Here, you can enter a bank balance
   for both your Current account and the Cash in Hand
   account if you so desire. You can also enter the balances for any new accounts that you want to set up
   here, if you have any further bank accounts that may
   be used in the business.

Figure 11-3: Entering the opening bank balance.

5. **Click Save.** A confirmation message appears on the screen saying that you've set up the opening balances correctly.

The screen now reverts back to the Financial Settings screen.

You can click the Banking icon to see a balance against the accounts for which you entered opening balances.

Setting Up and Using Cashbook Bank Accounts

You may only have one bank account, but if you need to create another one, or create a Petty Cash account (which I recommend that you set up as a separate bank account), check out the instructions below:

1. **Click the Banking icon.** The Banking window opens up in Sage One Cashbook, as shown in Figure 11-4.

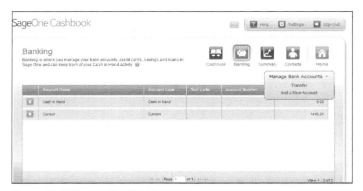

Figure 11-4: Viewing the Banking screen.

2. **Notice that at first two bank accounts are shown: Current and Cash in Hand.** (Flip to Chapter 7 for a description of the Cash in Hand account.) Hover over the Manage Bank Accounts button and a dropdown menu appears, as shown in Figure 11-4.

3. **Select Add a New Account.** The New Account window opens – complete the details for the new account.

4. **Click Save.** The New Account now appears in your Banking screen. A confirmation message appears saying that you've set up the new account successfully.

Editing your bank account details

Sage One automatically provides you with two Cashbook bank accounts: Current and Cash in Hand.

You may decide to rename the Current account with something more in keeping with your business. Here's how to edit your bank account details:

1. **Click the Banking icon.** This produces your list of accounts.

2. **Click the account you want to edit.** The Viewing Account screen opens.

3. **Click the Edit Bank Account button.** The window shown in Figure 11-5 opens. Complete the details as required.

4. **Click Save.** A confirmation message appears on screen saying that the account has been successfully updated.

Figure 11-5: Editing your bank account.

Return to the original Banking screen, and you can see that the amended account details now appear.

Deleting bank accounts

Provided that you have no transactions posted against a bank account, you're able to delete the account by clicking the grey cross next to the bank account name on the Banking screen.

Transferring money between accounts

At times, you're going to need to transfer money between your bank accounts. For example, you need to transfer some funds into the Petty Cash account.

You can also use the transfer feature to pay yourself some drawings if you're a sole trader, or when you invest money into the business.

You transfer money between accounts as follows:

1. **Click the Banking icon.** The Banking window opens showing your list of accounts.

2. **Hover over the Manage Bank Accounts.** Select Transfer and the Transfer window opens as shown in Figure 11-6.

3. **Select the bank accounts that you want to transfer money to and from.** Enter the date and any reference that may help you later.

4. **Click Save when you're happy that the details are correct.** A confirmation message appears to confirm that the transfer was successfully completed.

The bank balances have been adjusted for the transfer that you've just made. That's it, all done!

Figure 11-6: Transferring money between accounts.

Giving Credit to Cashbook

In this section, I focus on the pleasurable job of recording income in your Cashbook.

Cashing in with hard cash and paper cheques

In this section I assume that you operate a cash-based business and the money you receive is in cash or cheques (for which Sage One Cashbook is perfectly designed). Starting from the Homepage:

1. **Click the Cashbook icon and then the income circle on the Transactions tab.** You're presented with three boxes.

2. **Use the dropdown arrow, as shown in Figure 11-7, to select the appropriate payment method:**

    • Bank Receipt (perhaps a BACs receipt or a direct credit into your account).

    • Cash Receipt (notes and coins).

    • Cheque In Hand (someone pays you by cheque – see Figure 11-8).

Figure 11-7: Selecting the payment method for entering income.

Figure 11-8: Entering some cheques received.

3. Enter the Type of Sale using the dropdown arrows.

You can choose one of the following:

- Interest and bank charges.

- Other Income (income not generated from your normal sales for example, grant receipts, loan receipts).

- Sales (your normal day to day income).

Alternatively, if you aren't happy with the above options, you can click the Create New link and add a new sales type.

4. **Enter Payment date.** Enter the date that the money was received (as opposed to paid in).

   Note: If you've registered for VAT (whether standard or flat rate) you also need to enter an invoice date.

5. **Enter details into Box 3 as required:**

   - **Name:** You can enter a customer name here, if you want to record a cash sale against a customer without actually raising an invoice.

   - **Reference:** If you're recording bank interest, you can make a note of the interest period.

   - **Bank Account:** Select the bank account that you want to use. Note that if you selected a cash receipt, you don't have an option; the money is posted to your Cash in Hand account.

6. **Enter the total amount received into Box 4.** Check all the details you entered.

7. **Click Save when happy.** A confirmation message appears saying that the transaction has been posted successfully.

Bagging bank transfers

You may find that you receive payment via direct bank transfers or BACS. Here's how you record this type of transaction:

1. **Click the Cashbook icon and then the Transactions tab.** Select the Income circle.

2. **Select Bank Receipt in box 2 as your payment method.** Enter the type of sale and the date that the payment was received.

3. **Enter a reference in box 3 such as 'Childcare Vouchers received'.** Then select the bank account where the payment has been sent using the dropdown arrows provided, as shown in Figure 11-9.

4. **Enter the total amount received in box 4.** Make sure that you're happy with the details entered.

5. **Click Save.** A confirmation message appears saying that the transaction has been successfully posted.

Figure 11-9: Entering a BACs receipt.

Logging Expenses in Cashbook

Although I'd love to concentrate on all the money coming into your business, you also have to record the money that goes out! Here's how to record expenses:

1. **Click the Cashbook icon.** From the Transactions tab, make sure that you select the Expense circle.

2. **Select the Payment Method using the dropdown arrows in box 2.** You have the option to make a Bank Payment, Cash Payment or Credit Card Payment, as Figure 11-10 shows.

Figure 11-10: Selecting a Payment Method when entering an expense.

3. **Select an expense type.** For example, I use Wages and staff costs. Alternatively, you can add a new type by selecting Create New.

4. **Enter a payment date.** In this case I enter the date that the cheque was written. You can enter a supplier here by adding a name from the list or creating new.

5. **Enter a reference applicable to the cheque in box 3, such as the cheque number and what it's for.** Then select the bank account from which it's being paid.

6. **Enter the amount of the cheque in box 4.** Check that you're happy with all the details.

7. **Click Save.** A confirmation message confirms that you've saved the transaction successfully.

If you scroll down to the bottom of the screen, you can see that your transaction has been entered.

Again, and again, and again: Dealing with a recurring expense

If you have items that happen every month, you can set these up as recurring items as follows:

1. **Click the Cashbook icon.** From the Transaction tab, ensure that you select Expenses and then scroll down the screen to view existing payments.

2. **Highlight an existing expense.** The details show at the top of the screen as demonstrated in Figure 11-11.

3. **Click the Repeat button.** Doing so allows you to stipulate how often the recurrence takes place.

4. **Click Save to confirm the recurring transaction.** That's it!

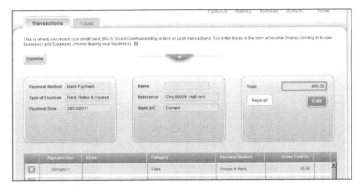

Figure 11-11: Entering a recurring expense.

Stop! In the name of Sage: Halting a recurring transaction

To stop a recurring expense, simply follow steps 1 and 2 in the preceding section and then click the Edit Recurrence button. This opens up Figure 11-12 where you can click Stop Recurrence.

The recurring expense is now stopped.

Figure 11-12: Stopping a recurring expense.

Give it up: Refunding expenses

The method for refunding expenses is exactly the same as for Sage One Accounts, and so turn to Chapter 7 for all the info.

Simply start off by clicking Cashbook and then Expense on the Transaction tab.

Recording Payments from Petty Cash

In this section, I assume that you follow my advice in Chapter 7 and the earlier section 'Opening and Using Cashbook Bank Accounts' and create a Petty Cash account as a bank account.

If you are yet to do so, please consult those sections and set one up now. This account replicates the float that you hold within you business, which means that you need to know how to record payments that you make from petty cash.

Here's how to enter payments made from your Petty Cash account (see Figure 11-13):

1. **Click the Cashbook icon.** From the Transaction tab, ensure that you highlight the Expense circle.

2. **Select Bank Payment as your payment method in box 2.** Because you created the Petty Cash account as a bank account, Sage One believes that you're making a bank payment.

3. **Enter the Type of Expense, using the dropdown arrow.** If you can't locate an appropriate type of expense, you can click the Create New link and add an expense type that's more appropriate to your business.

4. **Enter a payment date; that is, is the date the money was spent in petty cash.** Often you have a petty cash voucher or the actual date of the receipt that was given to you when you purchased the item.

5. **Enter a suitable reference in box 3 as indicated in the section above.** Also select the Petty Cash account as your Bank Account.

6. **Enter the amount of the payment in box 4.** Check that you're happy with all the details you entered.

7. **Click Save.** A confirmation message appears on screen saying that the transaction has been successfully entered.

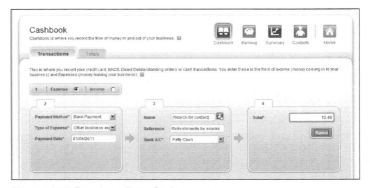

Figure 11-13: Entering a Petty Cash payment.

Wiping Away Mistakes: Editing Bank Entries

If you make an error while entering data into the Cashbook, you can rectify your mistake as follows:

1. **Click the Cashbook icon and then on the Transactions tab.**

2. **Scroll down to the bottom of the screen and you see a list of all the transactions you posted.** See Figure 11-14 for an example of income transactions.

Deleting bank entries

If you make a complete hash of an entry – and of course everyone does from time to time! – the easiest thing is delete the entry and start again. To do so, simply follow steps 1 and 2 in the earlier 'Editing bank entries' section, identify the rogue transaction and click the grey cross next to the transaction. A window opens up, and Sage asks you whether you're sure that you want to delete. Click Yes and the transaction is gone.

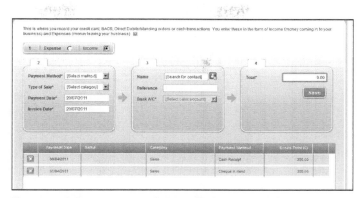

Figure 11-14: Examples of a selection of income transactions.

3. **Select the particular transaction that you want to edit, and those details appear on your screen, as shown in Figure 11-15.** Click the Edit button and alter the details as required.

4. **Click Save.** A message confirms that you've successfully edited the transaction. Your corrected entry now appears at the bottom of the screen, as shown in Figure 11-16.

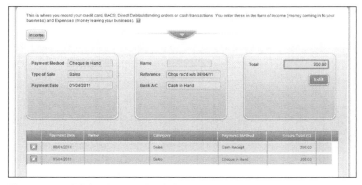

Figure 11-15: Editing the highlighted income transaction.

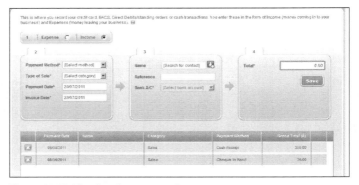

Figure 11-16: Viewing the corrected entry.

Paying into Your Bank Account

When you enter cash receipts and cheques in hand into Sage One Cashbook, the system automatically posts them to the Cash in Hand account. The Cash in Hand account is considered to be the place that you first receive your money, which may be cash in your back pocket or a cheque sent to the office prior to it being banked.

You then need to transfer the items showing in your Cash in Hand account to your Current account. Essentially, it is a two-step process; first you receive the cash or cheques into your Cash in Hand account, then you pay them into your Current account.

I recommend that you use your bank paying-in slips to enter the information. That way you make sure that you pick up all the correct details and don't miss anything out:

1. **Click the Banking button to identify the balances held in the Cash in Hand account.** See Figure 11-17.

2. **Select the Cash in Hand account by clicking on it.** The viewing account opens, where you select a date range. I select 1 April 2011–30 April 2011, as shown in Figure 11-18. A list of all the transactions posted between these dates appears.

Figure 11-17: Showing the Cash in Hand balance prior to transferring it.

3. **Click the Pay Into Bank button on the top right corner of the screen.** The Pay into Bank screen opens as shown in Figure 11-19. Notice that two boxes are present.

4. **Enter details into box 1:**

   • **Paying in reference** – Number on your payslip.

   • **Bank account** – Select the appropriate bank account. This defaults to your Current account if no other account has been set up.

   • **Date** – Date that you're paying the money into your account.

Figure 11-18: Showing a list of transactions entered into the Cash in Hand account.

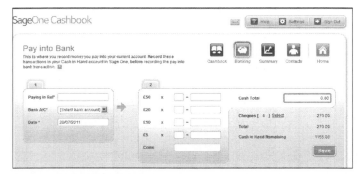

Figure 11-19: The Pay into Bank screen.

5. **Enter the cash and cheques that you're paying in into Box 2, just as you'd enter the information onto your bank paying-in slip.** You don't have to enter the cash details in so much detail; you can simply enter the cash totals.

   Figure 11-19 shows the number 4 after the word cheques. Therefore, Sage One identified four cheques that have been paid in to the Cash in Hand account and the value of those cheques is £270. The remaining cash value to allocate is £1155. These two amounts added together equal the balance currently showing in the Cash in Hand account.

   I enter the amounts paid into the bank using my bank paying-in slip. That way I can be sure that I've entered the correct amounts and the correct dates.

6. **Click the Select link to pay in a cheque.** The Select Cheques window appears as shown in Figure 11-20. Notice the ticks against all the cheques on this screen. Un-check all the cheques except for the one that you want to pay in. In my example, I select the cheque with the date 8 April 2011, which is what my payslip tells me.

7. **Click Save on the Select Cheques screen.** Sage now returns to the Pay into Bank screen. But now, Sage One has added up the cash and cheques for this payslip, and also tells you the remaining balance left in the Cash in Hand account. **Click save** when you are happy that the details are correct. A confirmation message appears on the screen saying that the deposit has been successfully made.

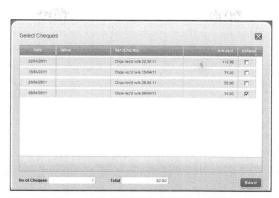

Figure 11-20: Selecting a cheque from the Cash in Hand account.

The deposit now shows at the bottom of the screen, and the system now waits to see if you want to enter any more deposits. Continue entering your information and ticking each payslip as you enter it. Eventually the balance in the Cash in Hand account equals zero, as shown in Figure 11-21 (after pay into bank).

Figure 11-21: The Cash in Hand balance is now zero.

Checking Your Bank Statements

To ensure that your records are as accurate as possible, regularly checking your Sage One Cashbook records against an actual bank statement is vital. You can do so at the end of each month, of course, but also on a more regular basis. This task is often known as 'reconciling your bank account' (see Chapter 7 for more).

If you have access to your online bank statements, you can reconcile as often as you like.

Reconciling your bank account entries

The Cashbook reconciliation process (called Checking the Bank) is very simple: just make sure that you have a copy of your bank statements in front of you before you start. A pen is also useful to tick off each item on your bank statement as you match it to Sage One Cashbook:

1. **Click the Banking icon.** The Banking window opens and you can see a list of your bank accounts and the balances of each.

2. **Select the account that you want to check by clicking it once.** Doing so opens up the viewing window.

3. **Enter the dates that you want to check.** I choose 1 April 2011–30 April 2011, as shown in Figure 11-22. You can also request previous checked transactions to appear by ticking the Display Previously Checked box. All the transactions posted to that bank account for that period now appear. Notice the checking box next to each transaction: at present, the boxes are unticked.

4. **Review each item shown on Sage One Cashbook and tick it off against your actual bank statement.** If you need to add any items of interest, click the Interest/Charges button as shown in Figure 11-23.

5. **Click Save when you've checked and ticked each item of your bank statement against Cashbook and you're happy that you've included all the correct items.** A confirmation message appears saying that your bank account has been updated.

Figure 11-22: Reviewing all the transactions posted to the Current account for April.

Figure 11-23: Entering interest and charges.

6. **Review your bank account again by selecting the same dates 1 April 2011–30 April 2011.** Notice that three items still remain. These items haven't been checked off, because they haven't yet appeared on the bank statements. The cash banked on 29 April hasn't yet cleared the banking system and is known as an uncleared deposit. Also, neither of the two cheques written out on 29 April has cleared the bank account, so both are unpresented cheques at the month-end (see Figure 11-24).

Figure 11-24: Remaining uncleared cheques and receipts.

Viewing a snapshot of your business

From time to time, getting a summary of your accounts is useful. You can easily do so as follows:

1. **Click the Cashbook icon, and then the Totals tab.**
   A new window opens, which allows you to view a summary of the Cash at Bank and the Cash in Hand account, as shown in Figure 11-25.

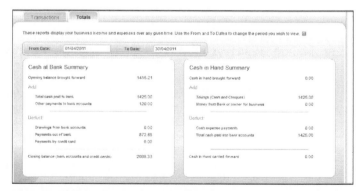

Figure 11-25: Showing a summary of the bank accounts and the Cash in Hand.

2. **Select the dates that you want to review.** I choose 1 April 2011–30 April 2011.

The total shown as Cash at Bank includes all your accounts; in my case it also includes a petty cash account that I created. The balance also has to take into account any unpresented cheques and any uncleared deposits that you may have entered onto Cashbook.

Running a Profit and Loss report

Sage One Cashbook can help you answer the most important question in the world . . . ever! Have you made any money? But don't bother looking until you're sure that you've posted all the transactions for the period and checked all your bank accounts for accuracy. After you've done so, however, run a Profit and Loss report as follows:

1. **Click the Summary icon.** A new window opens, showing a graphical representation of your bank accounts. You can see an example in Figure 11-26. Don't panic if it gives you an answer that you aren't expecting; the data is driven from current month data, and so if you're a little behind entering your data, and particularly if you've set up recurring expenses for future months, your figures may look a little misleading. You're better to run a Profit and Loss account using the link provided.

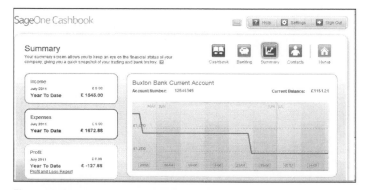

Figure 11-26: Showing the Summary window.

2. **Click the Profit and Loss Report link.** You're taken to the Profit and Loss screen, where you can select the

appropriate dates for your report. I use 1 April 2011–30 April 2011.

3. **Hover over the Download Report button to see options for Printable PDF or Export to CSV file.** I discuss these options in Chapters 6 and 9. I choose the Printable PDF option, as shown in Figure 11-27. Here I can see that Tots 'n' Toddlers made a profit of £672.12, which is much better than the loss that the Summary screen was trying to tell me as seen in Figure 11-26!

If you want to investigate the figures more fully, Sage One enables you to drill down to the next level of information. By following steps 1 and 2 above and then clicking on the figure you want to know more about, Sage One opens a new window which shows the activity produced for that particular item. For example, you could click on the Sales figure and Sage provides a graph showing the sales trends for the period and also detailed transactions that make up that figure in the report. (Refer to Chapter 9 for examples and screenshots explaining drilling down to the detail.)

Try to regularly print this information out, preferably at the end of each month, because doing so provides management information at its simplest but most effective level. You can see trends developing as you progress throughout the year.

Making a list and checking it twice

Here's is a useful checklist to help when setting up your Sage One Cashbook:

1. Create your appropriate bank accounts, renaming and editing the default Current account as necessary.

2. Enter your opening balances for each bank account.

3. Set up a Petty Cash account if required.

4. Set up the appropriate VAT scheme.

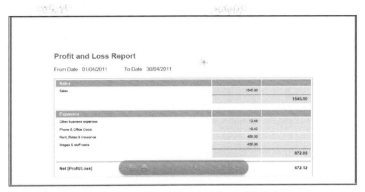

Profit and Loss Report

From Date 01/04/2011   To Date 30/04/2011

Figure 11-27: A Profit and Loss account for Tots 'n' Toddlers.

At the year-end, you can use an accountant to provide a more complete set of accounts, if you choose to.

Rehearsing with Sage One Cashbook

For the purposes of the questions in this section, I make the fictional company Tots 'n' Toddlers non-VAT registered so that I can demonstrate the differences on the screenshots between non-VAT registered and VAT registered.

1. **The Tots 'n' Toddlers play scheme has been running for some time.** Please add an opening balance of £1416.21 to the Current account.

2. **The only other account that Tots 'n' Toddlers operates is a Petty Cash account.** Please set up a Petty Cash account and transfer a balance of £150 from the Current account to the Petty Cash account on 1 April 2011.

3. **Please enter the following cash takings for April:**

   w/e 8 April 2011   Cash:£300

                             Cheques: £30

Payslip reference: 100021

w/e 15 April 2011   Cash: £285

                                 Cheques: £75

Payslip reference: 100022

w/e 22 April 2011   Cash: £280

                                 Cheques: £110

Payslip reference: 100023

w/e 29 April 2011   Cash: £290

                                 Cheques: £55

Payslip reference: 100024

You need to post the cash using Cash Receipt as your payment method and cheques using the Cheque in Hand as a payment method. Please post the income as Sales in the Cashbook.

4. **One of Tots 'n' Toddlers' customers pays using child-care vouchers, which means that the owner receives payment directly into the Tots 'n' Toddlers' bank account.** Please record this income as detailed below:

Date: 27 April 2011

Amount received: £120 paid directly into bank account from Childcare Voucher Services Ltd.

Reference: Jo Walker

5. **Tots 'n' Toddlers has one part-time member of staff and his salary for the month of April is £450.** On 29 April 2011 he's given a cheque no 000034. Please enter this cheque.

6. **Jeanette pays the rent to the village hall.** On 29 April 2011, she writes out cheque number 000035 for the sum of £400. Please enter the hall rent.

7. **Tots 'n' Toddlers makes payments for snacks and materials for craft projects from the petty cash tin.** Please make the following payments from Petty Cash:

1 April 2011   Refreshments for snack time: £12.46

3 April 2011   Paper: £2.99

5 April 2011   Craft materials: £7.43

8. In the first week of May, Tots 'n' Toddlers' bank statement arrives (see Figure 11-28). Please check your bank account against the entries you made in Sage One Cashbook to ensure accuracy of entries.

		Payments	Receipts	Balance
BUXTON BANK LTD				
Statement to 30.04.2011				
A/C Name: Tots 'n' Toddlers				
Sort Code: 23-12-34 A/C No: 12546345				
		Payments	**Receipts**	**Balance**
01.04.11	Balance brought forward			£1416.21
01.04.11	Transfer	£150		£1266.21
08.04.11	Deposit 100021		£330	£1596.21
15.04.11	Deposit 100022		£360	£1956.21
22.04.11	Deposit 100023		£390	£2346.21
27.04.11	Childcare Voucher Services			
	Jo Walker		£120	£2466.21
30.04.11	Balance carried forward			£2466.21

Figure 11-28: Copy of bank statement as at 30 April 2011.

Answering the Have a Go Questions

Check your work against the pointers here.

1. Figure 11-3 shows you how to enter the opening balance.

2. See Figure 11-4 shows you how to set up a new bank account and Figure 11-6 demonstrates how to transfer cash across to your newly created Petty Cash account.

3. See Figure 11-29 for an example of entering cash takings.

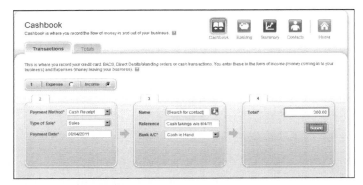

Figure 11-29: How to enter cash takings.

> 4. **Figure 11-9 shows how to enter a childcare voucher.**
>
> 5. **See Figure 11-30 for how to enter a cheque payment.**

Figure 11-30: Entering a wages cheque.

> 6. **See Figure 11-31 for how to enter the hall rent.**

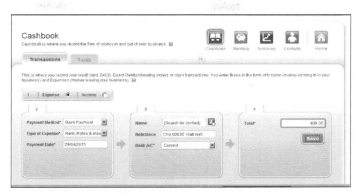

Figure 11-31: Entering hall rent.

7. **For the petty cash items, please see Figure 11-13 for the payment for refreshments.**

Figure 11-32 shows how to enter the paper payment.

Figure 11-32: Paying for some paper from Petty Cash.

Figure 11-33 shows how to enter the payment for craft materials.

Figure 11-33: Entering a payment for craft materials paid from Petty Cash.

8. **See Figure 11-22 for all entries in Sage that need to be matched.**

Part IV
Working with an Accountant

'Reading your accounts in the tea leaves is not really very satisfactory, Miss Jones.'

In this part . . .

I show you how useful an accountant can be to your business. I discuss the types of service that an accountant can provide and I also show you how you can find your own accountant if you haven't already got one. In addition, I explain the Sage One Accountant Edition and how your accountant can utilise it to provide you with an efficient and cost-effective accounting service.

Chapter 12

When the Going Gets Tough: Calling an Accountant

*A*s you read through the hands-on chapters and carry out the various exercises I provide in Chapters 5 to 11, you can't help but see how simple Sage One is to use and some of the benefits of using the software.

This chapter concentrates on something else that can benefit you; in fact some*one*: an accountant. So that you can decide whether contacting an accountant is the right decision for you, I describe how these professionals can help you and your business. If you do decide to take this route, I also offer some different ways of locating an accountant.

Clearly, this chapter is for those of you who don't presently use an accountant. If you already do, turn to Chapter 13, where I discuss the benefits of your accountant using Sage One Accountant Edition.

Nothing beats the expertise of using a trained professional, and so please be aware that the information in this chapter is intended only to guide you towards the available general business guidance. For more complex and specialist advice, I recommend that you find a good accountant, and this chapter shows you how!

Deciding Whether You Need an Accountant

A basic question that many small business owners ask is 'Do I need an accountant?' If you're starting a business for the first time and are quite happy to do the accounts yourself until you feel certain that you can afford the services of an accountant, that's absolutely fine. But do make sure that you're fully aware of the potential tax obligations of being the new owner of a business. Of course, these obligations very much depend on the structure of your business, but from the fact that you're reading this book, I assume that your business is, at present, small and run by an individual.

Whether you need an accountant or not depends on the complexity of your business structure. Therefore, the easiest way for me to assist your decision is to explain some of the things that an accountant can help you do. You can then decide if (or when) you need to use one.

In this section, I discuss the following ways in which an accountant can help you out:

- ✔ Advice on setting up your business.
- ✔ Self assessment.
- ✔ Company tax returns.
- ✔ Tax advice.
- ✔ VAT returns.
- ✔ Payroll.
- ✔ Year-end statutory accounts.
- ✔ Filing information to Companies House and Her Majesty's Revenue & Customs (HMRC).

Starting from scratch: Advice on setting up a business

An accountant can help you decide on the most appropriate structure for your business; for example, whether you need to set up as a sole trader, partnership or a private limited company.

Thinking of starting a business?

A very useful point of reference is `www.businesslink.gov.uk`, the government's online resource for business. A whole section is devoted to start-up guidance. When you log in to the Business Link website, simply click Starting Up on the top left side and you have access to information such as Forming and Naming your business and Taxes, Payrolls and Returns.

Going it alone: Sole traders

Most people set up as a *sole trader* because it's the quickest and easiest method. You can start up tomorrow, and all profits go to you. You need to contact HMRC to register as self-employed, and also complete annual self-assessment forms (see 'Helping assess yourself: Tax returns' later in this chapter) and submit them to HMRC.

One of the major downsides of being a sole trader is that you're personally liable for any debts that the business incurs. Therefore, your house and any other assets you own may be at risk if your business runs into difficulties.

The telephone number for the HMRC self-employed helpline is 0845-915-4515.

Cooperating with others: Partnerships

If two or more people are in business together, your accountant may suggest that you form a *partnership* (of which several types exist).

The common features of all types of partnerships are that the partners share the risks and rewards between them. So all income is split equally, unless the partnership agreement states otherwise. Your accountant can advise the best type of partnership to form, which dictates the level of liability that you have for the debts of the business.

The downside to partnerships is that you have a lot more legal paperwork to complete, and so really need to seek the advice of a solicitor before you go ahead and start trading.

Limiting the risks: Private limited companies

Your accountant may advise you to form a private limited company. A lot more administration and paperwork is involved with running a limited company, and so employing an accountant is very helpful, because she can guide you through the maze of financial and legal obligations that you need to adhere to. You must register the company with Companies House and advise them of the directors and company secretary using specific forms available on the Companies House website (www.companieshouse.gov.uk). You need to file the accounts annually and submit an annual return to Companies House.

A limited company is a separate legal entity and therefore the funds used to create the company are entirely separate from the personal finances of its owners (unless the director of the company gives a personal guarantee for a bank loan).

A useful source of information is the Companies House Cardiff Information Centre: 0303-123-4500.

Helping assess yourself: Tax returns

If you don't feel confident about preparing a tax return yourself, an accountant can help you to complete an online or paper tax return and then send those details to HMRC.

You need to submit a tax return if you're self-employed or a director of a business. The tax return involves providing information about your turnover and associated business expenses and profits, including any tax allowance and reliefs that you many want to claim.

The Business Link website (www.businesslink.gov.uk) contains more details about who needs to complete a tax return.

You face penalties for late submission of tax returns, and so ensure that you're aware of all deadlines and allow yourself plenty of time to prepare the information.

Dealing with company tax returns

Private limited companies (check out the earlier section 'Limiting the risks: Private limited companies') need to submit company tax returns (CT600), so that you can calculate the corporation tax that your business needs to pay to HMRC. Corporation tax is calculated by taking your company's pre-tax profits and adjusting them to arrive at taxable profits.

This area is where the expertise of an accountant becomes invaluable. If you do feel confident enough to do this yourself, you can find CT600 guides to help you complete the form on both the Business Link and HMRC websites (www.business link.gov.uk and www.hmrc.gov.uk).

Advising on tax

If you have less than straightforward tax affairs, an accountant can (often easily) sort them out for you.

Paying an accountant to handle your complicated tax affairs is money well spent. Tax-efficient planning is almost certain to save you money in the longer term.

Submitting VAT returns

Although, as a business owner, you may be quite happy to enter your day-to-day business transactions into Sage One Accounts and reconcile the bank account to keep a check on cash flow, you may be less confident (or indeed not have the time) to submit the business's VAT return. In which case, you'll be glad to that many accountants offer this service, but they probably want to do your year-end accounts or tax affairs as well.

This service is made particularly simple when your accountant subscribes to Sage One Accountant Edition (check out Chapter 13 for more details). She can do your VAT return for you, whether you subscribe to the Sage One Accounts or Cashbook.

Operating the payroll

If you have employees within your business, you have to operate some sort of payroll system.

Although you can do this task yourself, you need to become
aware of all the necessary payroll deadlines, particularly relat-
ing to the year-end. You also need to submit specific year-end
reports to HMRC and penalties are incurred for late submission.

Some small businesses find it easier and sometimes cheaper
to employ the services of a payroll bureau. These are usually
run by an accountant, who can provide your payroll service
as a standalone feature.

Note: Sage have indicated that they may be bringing out a
Sage One payroll service in the very near future. At the time of
writing, no further details are available, but you can be sure
as a user that Sage One will provide you with all the information necessary to use this service.

Preparing your year-end accounts

You need to prepare accounts in order to submit the details
required for your self assessment tax return and/or company
tax return. You can compile these year-end accounts and tax
returns yourself if you have the necessary skills and knowledge, but employing an accountant takes away the hassle.
You can relax a little knowing that these items are being prepared by someone who knows what she's doing, who can do
the job much quicker than you and so ensure that deadlines
are met.

Note: Self assessment involves completing an online or paper
tax return to HMRC. You're required to submit income and
or any capital gains (achieved through the sale of assets) or
claim tax allowances and reliefs.

Passing these tasks to an accountant also frees up your time
to concentrate on your business.

Filing information to HMRC and Companies House

Some business owners simply don't like dealing with HMRC and Companies House. Perhaps they feel intimidated and lack confidence when talking to the representatives. In truth, these people are perfectly straightforward to deal with and are helpful when they can see that businesses are genuinely trying to be cooperative and provide the relevant details.

Accountants, however, are used to dealing with these organisations. They know the correct terminology and jargon to be able to find out accurate, relevant information quickly and easily.

Finding an Accountant

If you decide that an accountant can help you with your business affairs, how do you track one down and where do you start looking? Well, unlike gazelles, accountants don't gather together around the same watering hole (unless they have a favourite pub somewhere!), and so in this section I provide a few ideas for seeking out these shy but not so elusive creatures.

Listening to word of mouth

Also known as 'referrals', other people's recommendations score very highly in my opinion because they can give first-hand knowledge of working with the accounting firm or individual concerned. You can get an idea of price and reliability, too.

Ask your family and friends, any business associates or even your bank manager.

Using local network groups

As well as using general 'word of mouth', you can ask business people that you meet at networking events who they use as their accountants and whether they recommend them. Accountants themselves are also present at these types of events and they're happy to have a chat with you about your business and how they may be able to help.

Linking up with other businesses

The Business Link website has lots of useful information about how to find an accountant. You can read and print out a number of articles from this website: www.businesslink. gov.uk.

Enter the phrase 'finding an accountant' into the search box, and a number of articles come up with helpful information, particularly about the different institutes and associations that accountants can belong to.

Local sites for local people: Finding your chamber of commerce

Most towns have their own chambers of commerce with members' directories and regular network meetings:

1. **Access the website** www.britishchambers.org.uk.

2. **Click the link on the right side called Find Your Local Chamber.**

3. **Select your local region from the map that appears.**

4. **Click to see a list of local chambers in your area.**

5. **Click the appropriate link to get the necessary contact details and website links.**

I managed to access the members' directory for my local chamber and obtain a list of accountants with website links and contact information in less than five minutes.

Checking out business directories – with caution

You can gain access to numerous business directories via the Internet.

Be careful with some of these websites and carefully check the credentials and qualifications of people before you commit. If in doubt, pass.

Networking online

More and more forums are being created on the Internet and they offer a wealth of knowledge. You can find these forums by simply typing 'accounting forums' or 'bookkeeping forums' into your Internet search engine.

You're presented with a list. Try a few out and 'lurk' on the forums. This isn't as ominous as it sounds! All I mean is look, but don't post. You can glean a lot of useful information from these posts and see who's offering useful information for free.

The people who post are often running their own businesses and put their website links in their signatures at the bottom of their posts. They know that they can build up a level of trust between themselves as a regular contributor to the forum and the readers, which often leads to new business for them.

Accessing the Sage Accountants' Club

If you're looking for an accountant who already has access to Sage One Accounts, you can look up accountants on Sage's own website:

1. **Go to** www.sage.co.uk. In the top right corner click Find a Sage Partner. A new screen opens with a map.

2. **Scroll down the screen to find a couple of fields with dropdown options allowing you to enter your postcode and find your nearest bookkeeper or accountant.** A list appears with your nearest contacts in your area. You can then contact them directly.

Chapter 13

Collaborating with Sage One Accountant Edition

In This Chapter

▶ Taking a look at what the Accountant Edition does

▶ Sending an invitation to your accountant

▶ Allowing your accountant easy access to your data

▶ Naming accounts to gather more specific information

*1*f you already have an accountant – or after reading Chapter 12 decide to hire one – your affairs can be handled even more efficiently and quickly if the accountant can access your Sage One Accounts/Cashbook directly. For this reason, Sage produces a special version just for accountants called Sage One Accountant Edition.

This chapter focuses on how this additional service can help you with your business, including improved communication, quicker problem-solving and easier gathering of useful data.

I don't go into great detail because you aren't going to use this software yourself. I give you just a flavour of what your accountant can do for you when he has access to the Sage Accountant Edition service.

Introducing Sage One Accountant Edition

The Sage One Accountant Edition is a service only available to accountants. It enables your accountant to access your financial data in real time, which is particularly useful if you want a query resolved promptly.

More specifically, the service allows your accountant to do the following:

✔ Take a look at your data while on the telephone to you.

✔ Make adjustments in your accounts using nominal journals (useful at the year-end when preparing your accounts, and something that I describe in the later section 'I Name that Account in One: Nominal Account Activity').

✔ Interrogate your data using Nominal Account Activity. This facility allows him to look at an individual nominal code and analyse the transactions that have been posted to that account (I explain nominal codes in the later section 'I Name that Account in One: Nominal Account Activity').

✔ Customise your account by changing account names and creating new accounts so that they're more meaningful to your business.

All these things are discussed more fully in this chapter.

Inviting Your Accountant to Join the Sage One Party

When your accountant opens up his Accountant Edition, he has access to two types of clients:

✔ **Active Clients:** These are clients that your accountant has already accepted as Sage One clients. He has the ability to access such client accounts at any time.

✔ **Pending Clients:** These clients have sent the accountant an invitation to act as a Sage One accountant for them, and thus allow him to access client data via Sage One Accountant Edition.

Many clients are invited to use Sage by their accountant, but don't worry, it works both ways, you can easily invite your accountant to use Sage One.

This invite facility is available only to accountants who are already Sage One users.

If you know that your accountant isn't a Sage One user yet, no problem. Simply ask him to contact Sage on 0845-111-1111 and ask to become registered with Sage One.

When you invite your accountant (I describe the exact procedure in Chapter 2), he receives a New Client Invite email message informing him that you're inviting him to be your Sage One Accountant. He can then accept your invitation and you're both good to go!

Logging In to Your Financial Data

Whether you have been invited by your accountant to use Sage One or whether you sent the invitation, either way, he's able to access your financial data.

The first screen that your accountant sees is shown in Figure 13-1. It shows the following information:

✔ Your contact details.

✔ The service to which you're subscribed.

✔ Your financial details, including year-end date, VAT number and the VAT scheme you're registered with (if appropriate).

✔ A graphical representation of your bank balance – much the same as you see in your Sage One Accounts service on the Summary screen.

Running your VAT returns

With access to your business's data, your accountant can produce the VAT return for you, which is especially useful if you're running the Sage One Cashbook and are registered for VAT. You can't run your own VAT return in the Cashbook.

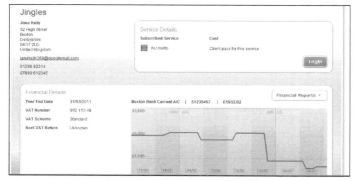

Figure 13-1: Initial screen that your accountant sees.

At the top middle of his screen is a button called Financial Reports. When your accountant hovers over this button, a dropdown menu appears with the following options:

- ✓ **Aged Creditors:** Basically the same as your Outstanding Purchase Invoices report (see Chapter 6), under a different name.

- ✓ **Aged Debtors:** The same as your Outstanding Sales Invoice report (see Chapter 6), again under a different name. This report shows the aged sales invoices, and the accountant can print it out in PDF format or export it to a CSV file just as you can.

✔ **Balance Sheet:** A snapshot of your business at a given point in time. Again, the same report as yours that I describe in Chapter 9.

✔ **Nominal Account Activity:** So useful that this facility has its own later section 'I Name that Account in One: Nominal Account Activity'.

✔ **Profit and Loss:** Shows the profit that you've made in a given period and is the same report as yours (see Chapter 9).

✔ **Trial Balance:** Allows your accountant to run a periodic report (showing the correct balance sheet balances at the period-end) as well as a transactional Trial Balance. The transactional report displays all the nominal codes for both the Balance Sheet and Profit and Loss but only includes the balance made up for each code where there's been activity in the specific date range entered. It doesn't include brought forward balances prior to this date range. (You can only run a transactional report, as I discuss in Chapter 9.)

1 Name that Account in One: Nominal Account Activity

The Nominal Account Activity facility, which is available only to your accountant, can provide some pretty useful reports. It allows him to name a category, such as Overheads, choose a specific overhead, such as Rates, and then view all trans-actions posted to that nominal account within a specified period.

Figure 13-2 shows a report generated on screen by Jingles' accountant, which shows all transactions posted to Rent and rates. The accountant can then export this data to a CSV file that he can open up in a spreadsheet to view. If he so desires, he can then design lots of pretty spreadsheets (and probably charge you for them!).

Figure 13-2: A Nominal Account Activity for Rent and rates

Nominal Accounts allows your accountant to help you customise reports and potentially produce some very interesting management information.

Here's an example. Jingles sells cards and balloons in the shop. Instead of just specifying all these items as Sales, the owner, Jeanette, asks her accountant to create some new sales nominal codes to allow her to report card sales and balloon sales separately. This data then shows up on her Profit and Loss and Trial Balance reports when transactions are posted to these nominal codes.

For example, Jeanette's accountant decides to create the following new nominal codes:

Nominal Code	*Description*
4000	Card Sales
4010	Balloon Sales

After Jeanette's accountant creates the new nominal codes, he has to journal, using double-entry bookkeeping, the correct balances across to each code. Fortunately, Jeanette has kept records of both sales of balloons and cards, so this allows him to be able to do that fairly easily.

Note: Journal means to move balances from one nominal code to another by way of double-entry bookkeeping. For example, you'd debit one code and credit another with an equal and opposite entry.

Creating Journals is another facility available only to accountants, because journaling requires a special knowledge of double-entry bookkeeping, something that accountants are particularly good at! Using Sage One, your accountant can complete year-end adjustments by way of journals to make sure your accounts are as accurate as possible.

After the accountant sets up Jingles' new nominal categories and codes, Jeanette can create invoices and cash sales using those descriptions as appropriate.

When Jeanette runs the Profit and Loss report again, she sees the new account codes appear – assuming, of course, that transactions have been posted to those accounts (see Figure 13-3).

Figure 13-3: The revised Profit and Loss account after new codes have been created.

Part V
The Part of Tens

'Take me to your Financial Controller!'

In this part . . .

The Part of Tens is the hallmark of the *For Dummies* series. Here I answer some of the difficult questions or scenarios you may find yourself needing help with when using Sage One. In addition, I include the top ten tips for running your accounts system.

Chapter 14

Ten Top Troubleshooting Tips

*T*his chapter offers you advice on sorting out those niggly little problems that can occur when you're processing data within Sage One. You know the sort of thing: something happens that you think shouldn't or doesn't happen that you think should. These are the recurring irritations that can drive you up the wall and your laptop out the window!

The issues I cover here are ones that occurred to me while writing this book; by no means do I cover all potential problems, just some of the more common ones that you may come across.

If you have an issue that this chapter doesn't resolve, you can phone the Sage 24/7 support desk on 0845-111-6611. They're always available to help you out, even breaking off from their lunch to answer a call from someone who hasn't turned the power on at the wall socket (just kidding!). You can also submit a query via the online form on the Help screen, and someone from the support team will contact you. This is also available 24/7.

Why do transactions that I expect to appear in my Current account appear in my Cash in Hand account instead?

When you enter a cash sale (perhaps as Other Income), Sage One automatically enters the transactions into the Cash in Hand account. This is because Sage One assumes that your Cash in Hand account is your 'back pocket' and as such you haven't yet paid the money into your bank account. You need to click the Banking tab and then Cash in Hand account before clicking Pay into Bank, as I describe in Chapter 7.

When I try to make a Petty Cash payment using Other Expenses, why does Sage One only give me the Cash in Hand account to pay from?

When you set up your Petty Cash account, in the eyes of Sage One it's another bank account (Chapter 7 has loads more on Petty Cash accounts). So when you want to make a Petty Cash payment, click Other Expenses and make the payment method Bank Payment rather than Cash Payment. You can then select the Petty Cash account from your list of existing Current accounts.

Note: When you create your Petty Cash account, you must ensure that the account type is Current. You can check this by editing the details of your bank account and checking that the account type is indeed current.

Can I do a VAT return within Sage One Cashbook?

No, currently no facility exists to do a VAT return within Sage One Cashbook. However, you can post VAT transactions and select the appropriate VAT scheme to which you're registered. Your Sage One accountant (if you have one) can then access your records and perform a VAT return for you (as I discuss in Chapter 13).

The Cashbook is really aimed at non-VAT registered businesses.

How do I record a cheque payment in Sage One?

On occasions you need to record a payment made by cheque to someone where no invoice is available, for example, when paying wages. To do so, select Other Expenses, Bank Payment

Options and then the Current account. Check out Chapter 7 for more details.

Put the cheque number in the reference field.

I forgot to put the cheque number as a reference on my bank payment – how can I correct this?

No problem. Click Expenses, Other Expenses and scroll down the screen to find the entry you want to amend. Click relevant entry and three boxes appear with the information you entered. You can edit the transaction and add the cheque number into the reference field and it then shows up as a reference against that bank payment.

Can I edit a payment made to a supplier or a receipt from a customer?

Yes you can, but you need to be able to identify the invoice against which the payment or receipt was allocated. When you know this, you can click the appropriate invoice and edit the details shown at the top of the screen.

How do I reverse a bank transfer?

The only way you can reverse a bank transfer is by putting an equal and opposite transfer through. You can't amend the transfer itself. Flip to Chapter 7 for all about the transfer procedure.

What if my bank reconciliation doesn't balance?

The first thing to do is check that you entered all the entries from your bank statement. You may have missed some items. Ensure that you tick the items off carefully as you go along, and identify any items that haven't yet been posted onto Sage. If this is your first bank reconciliation on Sage One, ensure that you've entered the correct opening balance for each account before attempting to reconcile. I describe the reconciliation process in Chapter 7.

Can I uncheck an item in my Sage One Cashbook?

When you're checking your bank statements against Sage One Cashbook, you can all too easily make a mistake and tick off the wrong item on Sage. As long as you haven't saved the screen, you can simply click the item again and the tick is removed.

If you find that you've incorrectly ticked an item and then saved the screen, you can either edit the transaction and re-save, which un-reconciles it, or delete the transaction and re-enter it. This has the effect of un-reconciling the item, because it no longer exists!

Can I change my VAT scheme?

Yes you can, but I advise you to consult your accountant first.

Never change your VAT scheme part way through a month; wait until the end of the quarter if possible and reconcile those items before changing schemes.

Although Sage One allows you to change the details of your VAT scheme at any time, it applies the changes only when the last VAT return in the previous VAT scheme has been completed.

You can change the scheme by clicking Settings, Financial Settings and then the Change link (next to the VAT scheme). Doing so opens up the Manage VAT Schemes window.

Sage has a help article that you're encouraged to read before you go ahead and make any changes. Click the little question mark icon to access the Help screen. Chapter 8 also has lots more on VAT.

Chapter 15

Ten Ways to Run Your Accounts System Effectively

In This Chapter

▶ Keeping track of your debtors

▶ Making sure you pay your creditors

▶ Reconciling your bank accounts

▶ Setting up efficient filing solutions

*R*unning your own business certainly isn't easy, and can at times be worrying, frustrating and exhausting. Using Sage One Accounts at least helps to take some of the strain of managing the financials off you. But you don't want to negate these advantages by then making things harder for yourself in other ways, such as filing haphazardly, neglecting the paperwork and losing track of bills and invoices.

In this chapter, I provide ten easy ways to make life just that little bit easier for you (and who would want it otherwise?).

Bank Your Cash Regularly

Cash is vital in any business, and so you need to be prepared to bank your cash on a regular basis. Choose a bank that's easy to get to and has banking hours that suit. Having the facility to bank cash in deposit boxes when the queues are too long at lunch time is invaluable when you're short of time.

Monitor Customers that Haven't Paid

This advice applies mainly when you sell goods on credit. You need to ensure that your cash is rolling in on a timely basis, so that you can avoid paying overdraft charges on your bank account. Your debtors may not be quite as fastidious at paying their suppliers as you are, and so be prepared to make a few phone calls.

Use Sage One Accounts to view your Summary screen and see who your top 5 unpaid bills are with (and hope that they aren't the same people every time!). You also have the ability to run the Outstanding Sales Invoice report, which I describe in Chapter 6. From this report, you can easily see who owes you money and get straight on the phone and chase them up.

Check Your Cash Flow

Cash flow is the life blood of any business. You can be unprofitable and still survive (for a while . . .), but running out of cash usually signifies the end of your business.

Make sure that you have access to your bank accounts online and can printout a bank statement at any time. This ability ensures that you can check your bank balance regularly and that you have enough cash to continue.

If you believe that you're going to run out of cash, but the situation seems temporary, you're much better equipped to discuss an overdraft with your bank manager if you go armed with your cash flow information.

With Sage One Accounts and Cashbook, you can check and reconcile your bank account (which I discuss in Chapter 7). Try to do so at least monthly, thereby making it part of your monthly accounting routine.

Keep on Top of Supplier Payments

As well ensuring that your debtors are paying you on time, you also need to make sure that you're paying your suppliers on time. Bad feeling on the part of a supplier who's not paid on time leads to future supplier problems. You want to build a strong team of suppliers who you can rely on to send goods at a moment's notice – just in case that big order comes in and needs to be fulfilled quickly.

You can easily see who needs to be paid by running your Outstanding Purchase Invoice report in Sage One Accounts (as I show in Chapter 6). This report allows you to see who's owed money and for how long.

You may decide to pay all suppliers who've sent invoices more than 30 days ago. Most business people use the Outstanding Purchase Invoice report as a basis for deciding which suppliers are going on the next payment run. Just remember that good working relationships are built on trust and paying your bills on time!

Maintain an Accurate Petty Cash System

Petty cash is notoriously difficult to keep under control, particularly if more than one person works in your business. I show you how to set up a separate Petty Cash account in Sage One Accounts and Sage One Cashbook in Chapters 7 and 11, respectively.

Regularly check that the balance in your Sage One Petty Cash account is the same as the cash balance in your petty cash 'tin'. If the amounts don't tally, make sure that you've entered all your receipts correctly and accounted for all expenditure. By checking the balance regularly you pick up any errors quickly and can rectify them more easily.

Store All Your Receipts

This piece of advice should really go without saying: always keep all your business-related receipts. If you don't, you're missing vital information when preparing your accounts.

If you're VAT registered, you can't claim back VAT on receipts you've lost or forgotten to put on the system. Valid VAT receipts are required for your VAT return preparation and you need to keep them for at least seven years to satisfy HMRC requirements – just in case you have a future VAT inspection and need to provide evidence of your receipts to HMRC.

Reconcile Your Bank Accounts Regularly

By reconciling your bank accounts on a regularly basis (at least once a month), you ensure that your accounting records are as accurate as possible. You know that you've accounted for all items of income and expenditure for your business and this information can then be handed across to your accountant to prepare accurate year-end accounts using your information as a sound basis.

Of course, your accountant needs to make other adjustments to your accounts (such as depreciation, possibly stock adjustments and payroll journals if required), but if the basic information is accurate, he doesn't have to spend time doing it himself and thus incurring more fees for your business.

Discover the Benefits of Easy-to-Use Filing Systems

File all your invoices so that you can find them quickly in the event of a query. As I mention in Chapter 5, rather than filing my invoices in alphabetical order, I give each invoice a sequential number. That way, they're all filed in one lever arch file and are extremely easy to find. I use the sequential number in the Sage One Reference field when entering the data for my purchase invoices.

Make Full Use of Checklists

I'm a big fan of checklists, particularly for bookkeeping and accounting. If you have several different jobs on the go, you can use checklists to great effect. I use one that shows me my monthly accounting tasks that need completing. As I perform each task, I tick it off the list for that month. I can see at a glance what I have and haven't done, which is really useful if you're constantly picking up and putting down your work.

Another useful area for checklists is when you're performing your monthly or weekly payroll duties. You can tick off each task as you perform it and you know exactly where you are when you return to your job.

Report in a Timely Fashion

Knowing your deadlines for reporting requirements, particularly with regard to HMRC and Companies House, is vitally important. To help, keep a diary system that reminds you of your statutory requirements for filing information to all the relevant bodies.

If you have an accountant, he reminds you of your deadlines and chivvies you along if needs be.

Appendix

Glossary

● ●

*A*lthough I don't use all these terms in this book, you certainly find them used regularly in the business world. So here's a quick reminder of what they mean.

Note: A term in bold in a definition indicates that an entry exists for that term elsewhere in the Glossary.

Aged Creditors report: A report showing all balances owed to **creditors** categorised into debts owed for 30 days, 60 days and 90 days and older.

Aged Debtors report: A report showing all outstanding balances owed to a business, categorised into amounts owed for 30 days, 60 days, 90 days and older.

Asset: An item that a business owns for use within the business (see **current asset** and **fixed asset**).

Balance Sheet: A financial report that shows a snapshot of the financial status of a business at a point in time. It identifies the business's **assets** and **liabilities** and shows how they've been funded through **retained profits** or invested **capital.**

Capital: Money invested into a business by owners or shareholders.

Cash flow: The amount of cash flowing in and out of a business.

Cash in Hand: An account that Sage One uses to receive cheques and cash. The money can then be transferred to the Bank Current account by using the Pay into Bank feature.

Chart of Accounts: A list of all the **nominal accounts** used to analyse **assets, liabilities, income** and **expenses.** It drives the format of the **Profit and Loss account** and the **Balance Sheet.**

Cost: Items of expense in the accounts, such as wages costs (see also **direct costs**).

Credit: A bookkeeping entry that increases the value of a **liability** or **income** and decreases the value of an **asset** or **expense**; always shown on the right side of a **nominal journal.**

Creditor: A person or company to whom a business owes money.

Creditor ledger: See **supplier ledger.**

Customer ledger: A ledger that holds all the individual customer accounts and their balances: also known as the **debtor ledger.**

Current asset: An **asset** with a lifespan of 12 months or less, such as stock, debtors and cash. A current asset can be liquidated reasonably quickly.

Debit: A bookkeeping entry that increases the value of an **asset** or **expense** and decreases the value of a **liability** or **income.**

Debtor: A person or company who owes the business money.

Debtor ledger: See **customer ledger.**

Depreciation: An accounting tool used to reduce gradually the value of a **fixed asset.**

Direct cost: A cost that can be directly attributed to the manufacturing of a product.

Double-entry bookkeeping: An accounting method that records each transaction twice. Every debit entry has a corresponding credit entry. Using two entries helps balance the books.

Expense: A cost incurred as a result of doing **revenue-**generating business activities.

Fixed asset: An item owned by the business that has a useful longer life than 12 months.

Gross profit: Revenue less **direct costs.**

Income: The amount of money received for goods and/or services provided.

Liability: An amount the business owes (see **long term liability; short term liability**).

Liquidate: To redeem an **asset** for cash.

Long term liability: A **liability** the business owes for a period longer than 12 months – a mortgage for example.

Net profit: Revenue less **direct costs** and **overheads**, including **depreciation** and taxes; also known as the bottom line.

Nominal account: An account to which every item of **income, expense, asset** and **liability** is posted.

Nominal journal: In years gone by, a leather-bound journal. Nowadays, computers have replaced the traditional journal and a computerised journal entry screen is used to transfer values between **nominal accounts** by using **double-entry bookkeeping**. This feature is available in Sage One Accountant Edition.

Nominal ledger: The ledger that includes balances and activities for all the **nominal accounts** used to run the business. The nominal ledger contains all the transactions that the business has ever made.

Overheads: An **expense** that can't be directly matched to a product or service that the business provides. Electricity and telephone costs are examples of overheads.

Outstanding lodgement: A deposit or receipt entered in the company's books that hasn't yet cleared the banking system. This term is used when preparing a bank **reconciliation**.

Profit and Loss account: A financial statement that shows the sales **revenue** less direct costs and **overheads** and arrives at the net profit or loss of a business for a specific period in time.

Reconciliation: To resolve differences. A business would normally perform a bank reconciliation, which involves checking the bank statement to the actual entries found in Sage One. The differences between the two would need to be resolved, for example, items not currently shown in Sage One, but seen on the bank statement would have to be entered.

Retained profit: Profit from a prior period reinvested in the business for a future growth.

Revenue: See **Income.**

Sales revenue: The net value of a business's sales invoices.

Short term liability: An amount owed for a period of less than 12 months.

Supplier ledger: A ledger that holds all the individual supplier accounts and their balances; also known as the **creditor ledger.**

Unpresented cheque: A cheque written out and entered into the bookkeeping system that hasn't yet cleared the bank account. Unpresented cheques show as outstanding items remaining to be reconciled after a bank **reconciliation** is complete.

VAT: Value-added-tax. A tax due on purchases of most goods and services supplied by UK businesses and those in the Isle of Man. VAT is collected on business transactions, imports and acquisitions.

Index

DUMMIES

Making Everything Easier! ™

UK editions

BUSINESS

Bookkeeping
DUMMIES
978-0-470-97626-5

Leadership
DUMMIES
978-0-470-97211-3

Starting & Running a Business
ALL-IN-ONE
DUMMIES
978-1-119-97527-4

REFERENCE

British Politics
DUMMIES
978-0-470-68637-9

DIY
DUMMIES
978-0-470-97450-6

Researching Your Family History Online
DUMMIES
978-0-470-74535-9

HOBBIES

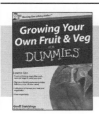

Growing Your Own Fruit & Veg
DUMMIES
978-0-470-69960-7

Allotment Gardening
DUMMIES
978-0-470-68641-6

Electronics
DUMMIES
978-0-470-68178-7

Asperger's Syndrome For Dummies
978-0-470-66087-4

Basic Maths For Dummies
978-1-119-97452-9

Boosting Self-Esteem For Dummies
978-0-470-74193-1

British Sign Language
For Dummies
978-0-470-69477-0

Cricket For Dummies
978-0-470-03454-5

Diabetes For Dummies, 3rd Edition
978-0-470-97711-8

English Grammar For Dummies
978-0-470-05752-0

Flirting For Dummies
978-0-470-74259-4

IBS For Dummies
978-0-470-51737-6

Improving Your Relationship
For Dummies
978-0-470-68472-6

Keeping Chickens For Dummies
978-1-119-99417-6

Lean Six Sigma For Dummies
978-0-470-75626-3

Management For Dummies,
2nd Edition
978-0-470-97769-9

Neuro-linguistic Programming
For Dummies, 2nd Edition
978-0-470-66543-5

Nutrition For Dummies, 2nd Edition
978-0-470-97276-2

**Available wherever books are sold. For more information or to order direct go to
www.wiley.com or call +44 (0) 1243 843291**

UK editions

SELF–HELP

978-0-470-66541-1

978-1-119-99264-6

978-0-470-66086-7

STUDENTS

978-0-470-68820-5

978-0-470-74711-7

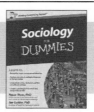

978-1-119-99134-2

HISTORY

978-0-470-68792-5

978-0-470-74783-4

978-0-470-97819-1

Origami Kit For Dummies
978-0-470-75857-1

Overcoming Depression For Dummies
978-0-470-69430-5

Positive Psychology For Dummies
978-0-470-72136-0

PRINCE2 For Dummies, 2009 Edition
978-0-470-71025-8

Project Management For Dummies
978-0-470-71119-4

Psychometric Tests For Dummies
978-0-470-75366-8

Reading the Financial Pages
For Dummies
978-0-470-71432-4

Rugby Union For Dummies, 3rd Edition
978-1-119-99092-5

Sage 50 Accounts For Dummies
978-0-470-71558-1

Self-Hypnosis For Dummies
978-0-470-66073-7

Study Skills For Dummies
978-0-470-74047-7

Teaching English as a Foreign Language
For Dummies
978-0-470-74576-2

Time Management For Dummies
978-0-470-77765-7

Training Your Brain For Dummies
978-0-470-97449-0

Work-Life Balance For Dummies
978-0-470-71380-8

Writing a Dissertation For Dummies
978-0-470-74270-9

Available wherever books are sold. For more information or to order direct go to www.wiley.com or call +44 (0) 1243 843291

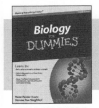

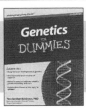

FOR DUMMIES

Helping you expand your horizons and achieve your potential

COMPUTER BASICS

Laptops
DUMMIES

978-0-470-57829-2

PCs
DUMMIES

978-0-470-61454-9

Windows 7
DUMMIES

978-0-470-49743-2

DIGITAL PHOTOGRAPHY

Digital Photography
DUMMIES

978-0-470-25074-7

Digital SLR Photography
DUMMIES

978-0-470-76878-5

Nikon D3100
DUMMIES

978-1-118-00472-2

MICROSOFT OFFICE 2010

Office 2010
DUMMIES

978-0-470-48998-7

Office 2010
For Seniors
DUMMIES

978-0-470-58302-9

Excel 2010
DUMMIES

978-0-470-48953-6

Access 2010 For Dummies
978-0-470-49747-0

Android Application Development
For Dummies
978-0-470-77018-4

AutoCAD 2011 For Dummies
978-0-470-59539-8

C++ For Dummies, 6th Edition
978-0-470-31726-6

Computers For Seniors For Dummies,
2nd Edition
978-0-470-53483-0

Dreamweaver CS5 For Dummies
978-0-470-61076-3

iPad For Dummies 2nd Edition
978-1-118-02444-7

Macs For Dummies, 11th Edition
978-0-470-87868-2

Mac OS X Snow Leopard For Dummies
978-0-470-43543-4

Photoshop CS5 For Dummies
978-0-470-61078-7

Photoshop Elements 9 For Dummies
978-0-470-87872-9

Search Engine Optimization
For Dummies, 4th Edition
978-0-470-88104-0

The Internet For Dummies,
12th Edition
978-0-470-56095-2

Visual Studio 2010 All-In-One
For Dummies
978-0-470-53943-9

Web Analytics For Dummies
978-0-470-09824-0

Word 2010 For Dummies
978-0-470-48772-3

WordPress For Dummies, 4th Edition
978-1-118-07342-1

Available wherever books are sold. For more information or to order direct go to
www.wiley.com or call +44 (0) 1243 843291

Printed and bound by CPI Group (UK) Ltd, Croydon, CR0 4YY